DON'T BE A SCHMECKLE!

Don't Be A Schmeckle!

By

Bruce Borenstein

Copyright © 2018

Printed in the United States of America

Printed Paperback   978-1-63039-113-3
e-Book - ePub   978-1-63039-114-0
e-Book - .mobi   978-1-63039-115-7

Acknowledgments

With this being my first stab at publishing I have several people I'd like to thank.

First is Al Kushner. I met Al through his outreach to me in LinkedIn®, encouraging me to participate in his Speakers Bureau program. When we met, he told me that having a book would give me "street-cred" as a speaker. So I took Al's advice, and here we are. Thanks Al!

Next, C.K. Gurin. Cynthia helped me with the editing, formatting and all of the mini-Bruce Borenstein cartoons created by her team. Having never undertaken this before, her assistance was invaluable. Thanks, C!

A shout out to my step-daughter, graphic designer extraordinaire, Chelsea Jordan. A very busy lady who found the time to put her talents to work on my behalf.

Also a thank you to my son Mike who was instrumental in getting my website set up.

The Consumer Technology Association provided a platform for many of my experiences. The network I developed over my 30+ years of membership was the gift that kept on giving. Too many names to mention here, but thanks to all from the Association with whom I have crossed paths.

Last, and far from least, my wife Sheri. She has been my inspiration and pillar of support from the day I met her. Her encouragement in getting this book out was unwavering. Love you babe!

Don't be a Schmeckle
About that title...

It's not easy to come up with a book that is about using common sense to help with your selling efforts. "How to Sell Better" or the like, isn't going to get anyone to pick up the book, let alone read it. So, in keeping with my warped sense of humor and my Jewish upbringing, I came up with "**Don't be a Schmeckle.**"

(*Schmeckle* of course, is not to be confused with *Schmekel* the purposeful misspelling of which denotes the name of the all-transgender, Jewish folk punk band from Brooklyn, NY, a group particularly known for their humor.)

The definition of "Schmeckle" is "*a small member of the male anatomy, or, a stupid person.*" Perhaps both apply, perhaps neither. But, that's not the point.

The book's point is, to get you to look at, and learn from, this compilation of thoughts, tips, experiences, and the like that I've gleaned, tried, experimented with, and had, during my 30+ years of selling.

So, if you have gotten this far, I must have done a good job of coming up with the title!

Bruce Borenstein

6

Don't Be a Schmeckle!

Perfection is not attainable,
but if we chase perfection
we can catch excellence.

Vince Lombardi

Chapter 1

Lombardi Time

Chapter 1

Lombardi Time

What would a book about using common sense to help with your selling efforts be without leading off with Vince Lombardi? Virtually every business author on the face of the earth has included at least one Vince Lombardi quote in books on this topic, so we definitely have a consensus going. Lombardi had some pretty good ideas.

You know who he was, right? For those who grew up after his time and may not be all that that familiar with his remarkable legacy, Vince Lombardi was head coach of the Green Bay Packers football team from 1959 to 1967. Lombardi led the Packers to victory in the first two Super Bowls ever played and, to this day, he is still regarded as one of the NFL's greatest coaches. In his honor, the Super Bowl trophy is named after him.

Lombardi was known as a strict disciplinarian on and off the field, and he was an absolute stickler for being on time. In fact, if he called for a practice, you were expected to show up 15 minutes early. For him, being "on-time" wasn't good enough.

Lombardi knew that preparation in all facets of football, (and in life, for that matter) was one of the keys to success.   Arriving for practice "early" allowed every player to mentally *prepare* for the upcoming practice instead of waiting until they were already on the field, to engage and achieve the proper mindset.

The concept of always arriving 15 minutes early became known as *Lombardi Time.* To memorialize the concept, on July 30, 2012, a clock, overlooking Lombardi Avenue at Lambeau Field, where the Packers play and where Lombardi coached, was set 15 minutes ahead of the actual time. Occasionally strangers to the area wonder about the time discrepancy, and in some cases they wander into neighboring shops to ask why the clock appears to be running fifteen minutes fast. Those who already know, of course, understand the importance that Lombardi placed on details of discipline, and highlighted that importance with something as seemingly small as arriving early so as to be better prepared for what comes next.

So, what does being 15 minutes early mean to the selling process?

First off, it allows you to mentally prepare for the presentation ahead. In many instances, there's set-up required for your presentation materials. If you're only getting a 30 minute time slot to make your pitch, showing up at exactly the appointment time means that some of the allotted time will be used just in getting set up. And, what sales person doesn't want to maximize face-time with their buyer?

Secondly, it shows that you're not only respectful of the buyer's time, being a little early demonstrates your confidence, capabilities, and dependability. The worst possible message you'd ever want to leave with a potential customer is that you consider your time to be more important than theirs. But you would actually do exactly that, by showing up without being fully prepared to answer questions or, should the opportunity present itself, even close the deal.

Time is money, and in sales, you need to remember that your client considers his or her time more valuable than yours. They've set aside a portion of valuable time in their busy day to see you. You'll want to respect that.

If part of my customers' expectations included wondering what time I'd finally show up and get started, chances are that I might not get any more of their business. So, just maybe, because I give my customers a little more of my time while protecting their time, they'll recognize the fact that my word is good, I'm dependable, and that I respect them.

The Lombardi Time rule also goes hand in hand with the Boy Scout's Motto of "Be Prepared." This is actually one of my favorite exercises for attendees when I give seminars. I point out the pencil and blank sheet of paper in front of each of them, and tell them I'm going to give them a very simple problem to solve. They're going to imagine that they own a boat, and they're going to invite some guests to go fishing with them. (I'm a lousy fisherman but an avid boater who owns a 28 ft. Wellcraft®, so I came up with this)

After reading the problem details to them, I ask them to raise their hands and tell me roughly how many minutes they think they'll need to write a two column "To-Do" list. One column is for things to do on the day of the boat trip, the other is things they would want to do in advance. I'll look for a show of hands estimating how long they think it will take them to write that list, and then I'll give them that many minutes to complete the task.

Once they're done, we'll compare lists. The point of the exercise is to learn to look at situations from all sides, mentally evaluating what needs to be done, so that the task can be accomplished properly, and without screw-ups.

The Problem: Let's say you've invited a group of convivial business associates to join you on your boat for a day of fishing. One of the guests is a newbie to offshore fishing. You've got a comfortably sized boat with plenty of room for fishing and entertaining. The weather is expected to be perfect and the fishing report says that

14

dolphin or snapper or blues, or what-have-you, are biting at this time of year. You're going to tell your guests that they're more than welcome to bring their own poles and tackle boxes, but that you always carry extra fishing tackle on board, in case they either forget theirs, or don't have any. You've also told them you'll plan to supply lunch, cold drinks, and bait, so all they need to do is show up. You've told them you'd like to get an early start, and you've said what time you'd like them to show up at the dock.

Sounds as if you've got your guests pretty well organized.

But are you organized? You're the host as well as the captain. This is the reason for your two column list. On that list you'll write down everything you'll need to do, to buy, to get, to confirm, or to check status on. One column lists what you're planning to do the day of the excursion, the other column is what you'll plan to do a day or so in advance.

We're going to assume that you keep your hypothetical boat in good running condition and that you also have a toolbox on board, so don't worry about that part.

Think beyond the obvious, and make your list with your guest's comfort and safety in mind.

Once my seminar attendees have done that, then they can check off their own lists against these questions and observations.

Many items on the list will be perfectly obvious to some attendees, but for others, that same item will not even have crossed their minds.

So here we go…

Do you have the right number of life preservers on board in case the Coast Guard decides to pull alongside and say hello? They're doing that a lot these days.

If one of the guests is a novice fisherman, perhaps a little nervous to be that far offshore, a little reassurance could go a long way. If you have state-of-the-art safety equipment on board for example, you could casually mention that you have a fully stocked, auto-inflatable 8-man raft and an EPIRB on board. (Emergency Position Indicating Radio Beacon)

Speaking of emergencies, how about your first aid kit? Somebody always manages to draw blood somehow. When was the last time you checked it?

Is your radio in good working order? Did you remember to check the fishing report to find out exactly where the fish are biting, and do you have a chart or GPS that shows you how to get there?

Got some extra filet knives for when you get back to the dock, so that more than one person at a time can clean the day's catch?

Did you think to bring along a good size box of plastic zip-lock bags? Your guests will need something to put their freshly filleted fish in for transport home.

Here's another thought, when, exactly, had you planned to pick up your supplies? Were you going to do that on the morning of the fishing trip? Were you planning to stop by the grocery store on the way to the dock and have the employees in the deli section make a raft of sub sandwiches while you shopped for soft drinks, beer, water, chips and cookies?

You know you can call that order in the night before, so the sandwiches will be ready for pickup when you get there, right? Did you think to do that? Nowadays you can actually call your entire grocery *and* deli order in ahead of time. That saves a ton of time.

You can also pick up frozen bait in advance. Fresh bait, not so much, so that has to be another morning stop.

What about sunscreen? It's a safe bet that some of your guests are going to have forgotten theirs, and you sure as heck don't want a painfully sunburned business associate to blame a week's worth of sunburn pain on you.

While we're at it, do you have a few extra floppy hats on board?

Foam can sleeves for cold drinks?

What about spare sunglasses? The local dollar store is a great resource for a thoughtful host, and they open at 8AM. Whoops. Didn't you instruct your guests to meet you at the dock at 7AM? Better handle that a day or so in advance.

And by the way, once your guests arrive, you don't want to suddenly discover that you're low on fuel for the boat, so it's a pretty good idea to take care of topping off the tanks a day or so in advance as well.

I could go on, but I think you get the general idea.

Once your guests do arrive you'll want to be totally organized and ready to give them your undivided attention. If you've prepared properly in advance, which is to say, if you arrive early, unload the supplies, stow everything where it's supposed to go before your guests get there so they don't have to witness a last minute, disorganized scramble, you'll be remembered as the perfect host, everyone will have a great time, and your guests won't forget it. They'll be enormously appreciative that you thought enough of them to treat them so well, and when you ask for their business, they'll remember your attention to detail. They'll be inclined to trust you with the details of their own orders because they've seen you in action.

At that point I'll also ask the attendees if anyone had something on their list that the rest of us had forgotten.

This same plan of action can be applied to any business problem. Look at the big picture. Anticipate. Be prepared.

It's important to remember that in whatever you do, others are watching. They're learning from you. You might not realize it, but you're mentoring the people you come in contact with every day of your life. You're continually setting an example for others. It's like that imaginary fishing trip we just talked about. Your guests weren't overtly judging, but they were subconsciously aware of every aspect of that trip. You displayed competence, responsibility, thoughtfulness, geniality, and common sense. You were also prepared for the unexpected, should it arise. That Swiss Army Knife caliber 8-man raft thing merits another badge on your be-prepared sash. You clearly care about your guest's safety.

That's a really good impression to leave them with. Do that in business.

Vince Lombardi once said, "They call it [what I do] 'coaching' but it is teaching. You do not just tell them...you show the reasons. After all the cheers have died down and the stadium is empty, after the headlines have been written, and after you are back in the quiet of your room and the championship ring has been placed on the dresser, and after all the pomp and fanfare have faded, the enduring thing that is left is the dedication to doing with our lives the very best we can to make the world a better place in which to live."

Lombardi was a pretty smart guy.

Be early. Be Prepared. Be a good role model.

Reply to messages within 24 hours. Even if you don't have the answer, always respond, "I don't have the answer yet, but I'm still working on it."

Chapter 2

Getting Comfortable With The Uncomfortable

Chapter 2

Getting Comfortable with the Uncomfortable

Scenario One: Your client is expecting delivery of an item which will be heavily advertised, and you had assured him of an arrival date. You just got word that you're going to miss that date.

Scenario Two: Your sales manager has asked you to start pursuing a new channel of business – one which will require cold calls.

Scenario Three: You've been asked to participate in a phone interview for a new opportunity.

What do these 3 Scenarios have in common?

A potentially uncomfortable conversation.

We've all been there, sweaty palms, butterflies in the stomach, racing heartbeat. So, how do you overcome that situation? Nike® provided a three-word answer. "Just DO it."

The only way to get comfortable with the uncomfortable is to deal with it enough times to understand how to handle those situations. But there's a great deal more to it than just that.

Scenario One: "Houston, we have a problem."

One of your best clients is expecting delivery of an item that will be the subject of a large advertising campaign, and you had assured him of an arrival date. You just got word that you're going to miss that date.

Fred M. is the Sales Manager of a busy, medium-sized manufacturing facility, and that's exactly the problem he's facing right now. He's just been advised that he has a major problem on his hands with one of his best clients.

He knows that he's going to have to address the problem with his client, and he plans to make notes on exactly what it is that he wants to say before making that call.

Fred M. wants to be prepared to anticipate different reactions from the client. He also needs to be able to respond without becoming flustered. His plan, in first writing out the entire situation, is a form of Cognitive Behavioral Therapy.

Setting out a problem in writing allows the mind to process the matter at hand differently. It assists the brain in taking a hands-on, practical approach to problem-solving. The goal of CBT is to change patterns of thinking or behavior.

Once the scope of the problem has been written out, Fred will then read it aloud to himself. The eyes often see what they expect to see in the written word. Hearing the words as you read them aloud however, draws upon a second set of senses which have the ability to identify subtleties that the eyes would otherwise have self-corrected, and therefore missed.

The very idea of setting this out on paper (or virtual paper for that matter) in order to come up with a clear, concise set of instructions for solving the problem, begins to feel daunting to Fred M. but he's going to do it anyway.

Fred is writing as if he were speaking directly to us.

FRED M: To start, defining an on-time delivery schedule had been predicated upon promises made by the then-plant manager, whose estimates were apparently designated as "far enough out, that we don't need to worry for 60 days."

Delivery had initially been scheduled to happen in 67 days, and I failed. I did not execute constant personal follow up other than in the form of a series of e-mails. My office admin had sent emails weekly to the plant manager, and had notified me of their transmittal.

However, she had neglected to let me know that there had been a breakdown in the process. We experienced a failure to receive the expected data, which would have supported our company's being able to meet the quoted delivery date.

The e-mail schedule initially designed, involved a weekly request for delivery and/or plant assembly status, along with any budget modifications. The e-mail schedule was intended to trigger a requirement for immediate action, should a shortage of any component develop, due to either sub-contractor delivery failure, or in-house manufacturing delays. In the event that there were cost items affecting the scheduled delivery, there was to be both an explanation, a new delivery date, and as needed, a new cost definition. As originally implemented, the plan was sound.

However, the plant manager had been abruptly terminated. His absence left many unanswered questions. Since his eventual replacement had been on the job for less than two weeks, forced to take the reins without a smooth transition, she too remained unaware of the massive iceberg looming large on the horizon. Although well qualified, the new plant manager had not yet been advised of, nor had she been in agreement with, the procedures and standards for which she could expect to be held accountable. She hadn't even had time to learn the floor operator's first names.

She had come to the company from a major manufacturing concern, with experience in managing assembly operations. She was without the requisite time needed to determine fit as well as function of each manufacturing quality control (inspection) for sub-assembly or, for the critical final assembly. Nor was she aware of the client's plans to kick-off a large advertising campaign.

In total, there was a very great amount of awareness that was lacking. The blame for misleading the client was clearly identified as belonging to sales management. Since that's me, I am confronted with a major informational problem, as well as a time-related action requirement. I MUST solve this dilemma quickly, or risk falling prey to being ousted from my own position.

Instinct and a personal moral code dictated a near-term response to the client, and full disclosure of the revised schedule – a major detail over which I had absolutely no information or insight, as to what might be the schedule fix.

For that matter, I couldn't even begin to visualize how a phone call or better yet, a face-to-face meeting might go.

Panic strikes. What to do? When to do it? Who can help? Who can I count on? Conversely, who do I think will be only too happy to drive a knife into my back for an opportunity to replace the disgraced. For many reasons, this is a horrific situation.

There is no simple answer. This is reality. The seriousness of the situation cannot be understated, yet it is clearly understandable. Unfortunately, the way out is not yet clear.

The planning of a step-by-step program can only come to fruition quickly; (1) If the groundwork has been properly laid, (2) There is total commitment, and (3) Involvement clarity for every single detail is absolutely firm. That logic supports even the unpleasant truth being told to the client.

However, there is a need to temper that truth with a plan capable of being understood by one and all, one which will serve this client's needs, and which can be implemented as a permanent safeguard for future promises made to both our clients and our management alike.

The end result has to be defining of a very real delivery date and include supporting data which assures that the date *is* to be believed. Each step in building a deliverable widget has to be clear and straightforward. There has to be (in the current case), an explanation for how and why, despite our otherwise logical planning, it did happen.

Step one is to meet with the new plant manager and to bring to her attention the potential harm that could occur unless we all pull on the same set of oars. Teamwork will enable us to move the boat in the right direction, thereby avoiding that pesky iceberg.

The assignment of blame could have been directed toward the departing plant manager, with a goodly share of the fault being blamed on my admin, who failed to immediately alert me to the potential of an impending debacle. It's possible my admin either didn't know of, or simply didn't register the importance of the plant manager's dismissal as it related to our own department. The problem with affixing blame is that there is a hang-over that can damage our company (and could adversely affect my personal future). The admin and departed plant manager are both subject to substantial relocation and reputation damage (me too). So it becomes necessary to NOT lay individual blame on anyone.

Rather, it must prove that a systemic, but correctable procedural problem is more palatable, and clearly advantageous as a recovery framework.

Clarity has been achieved. The immediate step is to call everyone on the plant floor in for a special meeting. The purpose of the meeting is to describe in detail to one and all, exactly what happened, and why it is so serious. The end result sought, is a solution that requires the commitment of each and every worker to deal with this specific problem as rapidly as possible.

It should be noted that this is a meeting where neither the new plant manager nor I are formal in attire or manner, but are on the floor with our shirtsleeves rolled up, and at the same team level as the people in production. We're being totally honest about all of the problems and steps necessary to meet the client's needs, and to arrive at a consensus plan for the future, that derives format with detailed input from the entire workforce. It is absolutely critical that the "final" plan be identified to top management as coming from the entire group, not just from me, or only from the plant manager!

The initial question has to be raised. What is needed to get the widget to the client as fast, but also as "right" as inspection can make it? Does it mean setting aside items that are being worked on now? Will that change other delivery schedules? Do we need overtime? Can that happen?

This is all crucial stuff. It has to be real. It must be sincere. It has to be the basis for future client liaison and for future involvement of the entire workforce to support sales and marketing. And, it means sales and marketing people must listen to the plant personnel, just as the plant people must listen to them.

The discipline and small stuff is absolutely critical. The project output has to be a date that I believe in, and one that I can sell to the client. It has to be a communication and functional plan, which is both clear and simple, so it becomes a part of the overall plant – sales and marketing commitment to serving the client.

That means a whole lot of extra effort. It means a bunch of listening to everyone else's input (some of which may very well not be valuable) and getting every single person in the plant and office both involved and committed to a plan and solution that they understand and believe each had a hand in developing.

I am glad that I'm not paid on a commission-only basis.

The following day:

In terms of the necessary telephone call to the client, since I am responsible to the client, I will assume full blame and accept responsibility. I will explain that my follow-up system had errors. The shortcomings have been identified, and then made known throughout the company, thereby assuring that we will not be faced with a recurrence. The proposed solution has been agreed upon at all levels within our company.

I have drafted a written plan which will be transmitted to the client for his/her commentary as to detail and completeness, in order to meet the client's functional needs. It must meet the client's need(s) because it has been based upon our confirmed facts and what little what we have been privy to of their own plans. As such, under the circumstances, it is as accurate as it can possibly be. Plus, it contains a detailed informational plan to keep the client alerted and fully on board.

At this point in my call, all that I can do by telephone is to extend my apologies for the error we made, again stating that my response is not a token or "quickie" effort. It is a sincere demonstration of the clients importance to us, and of our concern that scheduling details are implemented as paramount and on time.

My goal is to be in front of the client as quickly as possible with a workable arrangement documented. Depending upon the client's location and how rapidly we can develop the plan, I will be there on such and such a date and the Widget will arrive ready to go on such and such a date. I am going to have to tell him or her that this is what we have done; this is what we are going to do, and this is what I have expressed to our top management. It really is all that can be done and does not reflect discounts, non-payment and other incentives to ensure their continued business.

In point of fact this whole debacle really is my fault. I was aware of the plant manager's departure. I was also aware of the new hire. At no time however, did I roll up my sleeves, grab a clipboard and head for the factory floor to meet the new plant manager and check on the status of my job(s), and yes, that was "jobs" plural. The good news is that this mess has only affected one of them.

The bad news is that it has affected one of them.

And although my admin had faithfully sent status report reminders to the plant manager's email address, at no time did it occur to me (or her, apparently) to ask if there had been any status updates, positive, or negative, or a confirmation of receipt for that matter.

If my client asks, I will tell him the unvarnished truth and I will look like an idiot, but it will have been my own fault, and I quite assure you that it will never happen again.

Scenario Two: Your sales manager has asked you to start pursuing a new channel of business – one which will require cold calls.

Philip K. will be answering this one.

Cold calls are among my least favorite things, but I've gotten to the point where they no longer bother me as much.

Assuming that my expenses and costs are covered, and that my boss has not borne a long-term hatred of both me and my work, and is using this as a method of painless extraction, I will look hard at the newest widget to see if we are better off capitalizing the term (i.e. Widget) or keeping a low profile (widget) because it is expected to be used without general consumer awareness. For example, it may be a component of a far larger device, or perhaps there's a possibility it could be marketed as a free-standing item.

How useful is it? How reliable? Vulnerabilities to weather, changes in temperature, moisture, etc? Where might a consumer find it? In a store? Where, and on which shelf? Is it an online small item? Is it a large piece that can be ordered from a branded store, or is it an internet only item?

Does it fit into our current Amazon® SKU mix? Is it likely to be used by older Americans or young folk? Family oriented? Language sensitive? Gender sensitive?

All of the markets are different, thus having a panel of "experts" sample, handle, smell and/or taste while all are looking at the logical sale price point, as well as examining and opining on quality, likely longevity, and most certainly anticipated consumer appeal, all go together to determine the most logical (if not best) marketing or merchandising strategy to be followed for any marketable item.

Once the product (Widget) is assessed, defined and priced, the telephone cold calls can begin with a reasonable expectation of positive responses, depending upon the potential client. If (for example) the Widget looks to have Walmart® customer potential product appeal, then it becomes necessary to assemble a sharp design team armed with a well understood list of costs, suppliers and distributors, and plan to take them all to Arkansas (specifically, to Walmart's corporate headquarters in Bentonville,)

The cold call is supported by the panel's approval and by the supportive and salient fact suggestions. The buyers at Walmart may appear casual, but be assured that each is extremely bright and well informed. The new Walmart corporate headquarters in Bentonville has a tentative opening scheduled for somewhere around the year 2025. In the interim, the original building remains a sprawling, poorly lit facility with parking in hiking distance, genuine linoleum floors, and mounted fish on the walls. The 1950's aura almost seems designed to tempt unwary manufacturers into underestimating savvy Walmart buyers.

The time allotted for presentation is typically minimal and all of the necessary information needs to be ready and understandable. In all cases it is still crucial to have a fixed, simple approach. The actual "cold call" is a very constrained experience. It will be brief and to the point. No need to be nervous. Take away trial requirements, and it is a price and delivery discussion. Assumptions should be that Walmart® is very likely to be a margin limiting experience for a substantial amount of time.

But, there are viable alternatives such as Amazon® plus our company's own website, and now, we also have an opportunity to open an eBay® Big Commerce Store as selling options. 80% of everything that is sold on eBay is brand new. In April of 2016, eBay and Big Commerce announced a strategic relationship to enable Big Commerce merchants to seamlessly list their products and manage their inventory on the eBay marketplace, providing access to 162 million globally active eBay buyers. Sales success and demographic data can be shared from direct marketing, and our broader scope of online sales and can support the likelihood that it will do well in a brick and mortar environment such as Best-Buy®, Target®, and similar locations.

Home shopping sites such as HSN® and QVC® both now owned by Liberty Interactive after a $2.6 million dollar merger in 2017, may also be a viable marketing option. That would make the newly combined network the third-biggest in the U.S. by sales, behind Amazon and Walmart. If you can handle cold calls to any of those three, trust me, you can handle anything.

Forget the butterflies. You can do this.

Scenario Three: You've been asked to participate in a phone interview for a new opportunity.

Well, this is not butterfly in the stomach territory, but it certainly can be tricky.

There are two types of telephone interviews, scheduled and unscheduled. Most of the time you'll first be contacted by email first, via LinkedIn, Indeed or wherever you might have your CV listed and it will be someone specifically searching for an individual with your credentials or someone responding to your application.

Be a little wary of unscheduled calls without prior notice, unless you can verify who they actually are. Sometimes that call is from your own H.R. department doing a little amateur sleuthing to see if you're thinking of leaving.

If you receive a call when you're at your existing workplace, common sense and basic courtesy says that you should gracefully respond that you're in the middle of a meeting or on a rush deadline. Ask for their name and telephone number and ask them to send you an email with their name "and a little more information." Tell them you'll be happy to get back with them a bit closer to the end of the day. Make sure they use your personal email, not your company's email address.

If it's the call you've been hoping to receive and you're in a location where you can candidly respond, two of the things you can expect to be asked are, why you applied with them, and what you know about their company.

Do your homework. If you're on the road a lot, simply carry those notes with you, so that wherever you happen to be when the call comes in, you can whip out your cheat-sheet and answer those questions.

If you have questions you'd like to ask the interviewer, now's the time to do it. A serious telephone interview lasts about thirty minutes and if you get that far, you'll likely be invited to interview for the position in person.

There are three main rules for a telephone interview;   Listen carefully, then talk. Then listen carefully again. You'll be able to come away with a better sense of how the interview went.

If you really want to appreciate getting comfortable with the uncomfortable just take a look at how the Navy Seals teach that (and I pulled this from an INC mag article on motivation.)

One exercise in SEAL training is "surf torture." You link arms with your classmates and stand, sit, or lie in the frigid Pacific Ocean until your body reaches the early stages of hypothermia. During the initial phases of training, you do this daily. Then you cover yourself from head to toe in sand and stay that way for the rest of the day. You might follow this with running the obstacle course, weapons training, or classroom time, but you are expected to push the discomfort aside and stay focused on the task at hand.

There have been many times as a business owner that I have been in very uncomfortable situations. That could be a difficult conversation with a team member, a lawsuit, or dealing with a demanding board member. Discomfort comes in many forms. But the more you embrace that as a reality, the wider your comfort zone becomes. This boosts confidence and provides the tools for facing even larger challenges down the road. –INC June 2014

This surely has to be the ultimate in discomfort, but the lesson is a powerful one. It will add a little perspective to what you're faced with when the shit hits the fan in your world. Compared to this, your problem is a walk in the park.

Knowledge Is Power.

Know how your competition stacks up against you. You'll be in a much better position to understand where you fit in.

Chapter 3

Knowledge Is Power

CHAPTER 3

Know Thy Competitor - Knowledge is power

If you know how your competition stacks up against you, you are in a much stronger position to know where your own product line fits in.

I've always made it a point to analyze a competitor's retail space, both digital as well as their physical brick and mortar retail locations, to see what and where my competition is selling.

Marketing research is significantly easier to accomplish today than it was a relatively few years ago.

In 1992 there were only 26 websites in the entire world. As of January 2018 there were over 1.8 billion.

Mosaic® is the web browser that helped popularize the World Wide Web and the Internet. It was also the first browser to display images inline with text. Developed at the National Center for Supercomputing Applications (NCSA) at the University of Illinois Urbana-Champaign beginning in 1992, NCSA released the browser in 1993.

It hit the shelves that same year in a product manufactured by Mosaic licensee Spry, Inc. aptly christened "Internet In A Box®." The product was cleverly marketed in a brown cardboard box emblazoned with that name. Mosaic became the first web browser to win over the entire visionary portion of the public, and it was considered one of the "killer apps" of the 90's. Consider this; Today, finally, even the most reluctant of corporate adopters of new technology have grudgingly accepted the fact that this online marketing business might not be such a bad idea after all. For those of us who watched with fascination the transition from "Internet In A Box" to smartphones, we witnessed the warp speed equivalent of going from horse and buggy to supersonic passenger aviation in a plane that travels 100 mph faster than the new Concorde. (Scheduled to be in full operation within five years.)

Almost all major manufacturers have company websites, in most cases with a page devoted to where their products can be found.

On a manufacturer's website there's usually a link to a page entitled "Where To Buy" or similar, which typically provides the names of commercial resellers (Staples®, CDW®, etc.) along with a list of certified partners (Dell®, Lexair Electronics®, etc.) plus a list of their consumer retailers (ATT®, Amazon®, Best Buy®, Costco®, etc.)

From there it's a matter of checking those websites for location of brick and mortar facilities in your own sales territory, and then visiting those businesses in person to get a good solid feel of what you're up against.

For the details, today most potential customers will first hit the internet to do their homework and compare product prices and features. They'll also spend an inordinate amount of time on Google® searching for buyer feedback, operating instructions, and comments on customer service. They'll also head for YouTube® to view amateur demonstrations of the product and to learn how great or how totally lame the product is.

For both a manufacturer, as well as for company sales staff, actual consumer reviews of your competitor's products are literally worth their weight in gold. They're equally valuable to your own product development staff.

Online prices are generally less expensive than brick and mortar store prices, even with shipping factored in, so you'll want to remember to compare apples to apples when researching the competition. Depending upon the product, instant gratification, that is, allowing the customer to have it in hand today instead of waiting a week of so for shipping, often outweighs cost differential.

And that takes us back to brick and mortar retail product presentation.

If the store itself has steady traffic, and if the location is good, I'll want to verify where and on what shelf my competition's products are displayed.

I would then be able to create (or update) a presentation which focuses on what my product could do versus what that competitor could do, assuming identical real estate – thereby giving consumers additional choice, but better R.O.I. features my product might have that my competitor's product doesn't.

In some parts of the world, walking through a mall or down a picturesque street looking through the big shop window and staring at your competitor's displayed products doesn't really tell very much beyond the shop's location and the quantity of customers in the store at a specific time of day. Are these serious shoppers, casual browsers, or are they just dodging rain, blazing heat or bitter cold for a few minutes?

Real questions are those that can only be answered by witnessing first-hand what products are on consumer view and are displayed in an "idealized setting."

Comparing what products are being offered and seeing first hand how your competitors have presented their wares lets us evaluate their items against our products for product appearance (*that's easy*); for quality and price (*not nearly as easy, but a viewed opinion is important*) and, observing what their prospective purchasers seem most interested in, and what it is that they're actually buying. This is the critical determination and the information must be precise.

You have to be able to combine objectivity with overall observation – find out what is it about the product that consumers like or dislike, or if they have problems in use. This is where a combination of good eyesight and sharp hearing are necessary.

One way of getting immediate feedback is to stand in front of a shelf or a rack with a slightly lost look on your face, as if you were a customer. When approached by sales staff, you could ask general questions, "I'm a little new at this, my son/daughter, husband/wife, grandson/grand daughter told me they wanted/needed a such and such and I'm trying to figure out which is best and why. What do you sell more of? Why do people like that one? Etc.

Likewise you could casually engage another shopper in momentary conversation. "Excuse me? Do you happen to know anything about electronic widgets? I see so many of them on display here and I have absolutely no idea which one is supposed to be better, do you?"

"Spying" on the competition is a low cost way to find out what has to be done in order to establish whether your merchandise is equal, superior or (*worst of all*) inferior to theirs. Is our sense of "presentation" as good, as motivating for consumers as theirs? Do we seem to have an advantage or disadvantage? How can we take advantage of our product being more attractive to end users than our competitor's product?

If we are "better" then how, why, and what is the edge that we have on them? Does the customer know that we are better? Do they think our pricing is more desirable? Is it that we have done a better job (or are we worse) in literature and visual marketing clarity? Have we overstated our product's capabilities? Do they have a technical or quality advantage, or are we on the wrong course? Do they have an unstated marketing advantage over our products? What is it?

Since the actual product differences may be slight either favoring their product(s) or ours, differences may well be in an end-user's understanding or perception, rather than in physical attributes. This is important stuff. They have their sales and technical personnel tuned to a very specific set of "facts." Knowing what those facts are, is vital to our knowing what, and why they exist as competition.

Can you see what your competitors are doing without disclosing that you represent the opposition? Can you listen and observe what their end-users think, say and believe? Do you have a firm grasp on what your competitor's strengths or weaknesses are?

And, importantly, does *your* understanding make a difference in how your organization addresses the pitfalls it encounters in being a competitor?

Or, do they simply sell what they're told to sell without any particular regard for what you as a marketing specialist, see?

It doesn't matter if you are a manager or a rookie. The rules of warfare apply. Seeing, listening and observing with both an objective and a critical eye is necessary. All is fair in love and war. You are looking at what the competition does and you're looking to find weaknesses that your people can exploit. The objective is to win the customer and secure the loyalty of that customer for future buys. Second place isn't a goal. It is a manifestation of inadequacy.

It's possible that what might be done to aid in your product besting theirs has already been considered and rejected for a variety of reasons. Never assume you understand all the thinking that led to your company's decisions. You do not have all of the facts, nor do you know what caused anyone else to decide on this over that.

The issue that has to be in first position, is not "can I do what is needed?" or "is it simply too difficult a task to take on a competitive organization." Be practical. First on your list must be to separate your findings into things *you* can do, and those things that have to be done by others.

Is one of your goals to succeed in the organization? Consider it likely that you will be seen in a minimally desirable light. Presentation of your findings may result in interruptions, or resistance, or worse. Wishy-washy phrases like "If it's not too much trouble" or if you are overly cautious because you're afraid of being seen as ultra-confident without needed support backing, or if a co-worker takes credit for the detective work that you have done, or for the work you and he/she have done together, it's uncomfortable at best. You know the power of speaking up. But, you need to feel valued and worth listening to in order to speak with authority and presence. You need to be listened to.

This is a difficult chore but it's also very important. Can you approach this arena with minimal ego? Do you have to take credit for every step? What about the boss who will tell the world that he or she did all the work that you actually did, with the attitude that they as your superior are more deserving of the credit than you are?

So, do it yourself. Plan, think and write down a listing of all of the objections and resistances that are likely to confront your planned knowledge dump.

List all of the things that you see as deficient in your existing products and their merchandising and marketing. What things have the test groups discovered that have been ignored by decision makers?

Remember the Pringles® debacle a few years back when reliable Procter and Gamble®, the company that always "tested its way to the future" thought they were making, advertising and selling a better form of potato chips, a product that consumers were bound to love? Uniform sizes, uniform shapes, unbroken and neatly stacked in a handy tennis-ball style canister? They didn't listen to actual users. Their product didn't look like potato chips and it certainly didn't taste like potato chips. Nor were the chips broken and greasy, which users indicated was actually part of the appeal. But that's how they were being marketed, and it was one of the biggest product failures in marketing history. Losses coupled with industry embarrassment meant selling off a potentially exciting brand to a much less marketing-oriented organization.

As it happens, the public was absolutely correct, and no wonder they didn't taste like potato chips. During a court case in the U.K. some years back the actual ingredients of Pringles were disclosed. Only 42% of a Pringle is potatoes, the rest being wheat and corn flour, emulsifiers, fat and seasonings. Once internet wags got hold of that information they cheerfully speculated that additional components were sawdust and ground-up newspapers.

51

Of course, once the pain caused by erroneous product understanding had subsided, and management became better aware of consumer needs, they re-acquired the product and with today's very different merchandising, happily filled shelves with a product described as a "snack" available in multiple flavors, and not a potato chip at all.

All of this happened because of a failure to look at and understand the way a consumer views a product and then actually listening to consumer observations. Taking into consideration the consumer's needs, "wants" and product understanding, not only prevents errors, it provides direction for the future of product positioning, advertising and marketing channels.

As some of you might already know, my own background spans over 30 years in the global consumer electronics industry. As President and CEO of an award-winning company with cutting-edge products, I didn't just attend meetings and listen while my marketing division reported to me. I also made it a point to do my own homework.

That company manufactures and markets a product using patented bone conduction technology initially developed for military special operations and law enforcement. We introduced it for sport, mobile, and everyday use, music, phone, gaming and targeted listening enhancement. An ambient noise cancellation feature was particularly helpful for individuals who are autistic.

As our company literature pointed out, "through a suite of proprietary audio technologies and the only completely open-ear design, the headphones deliver premium stereo sound, and a promise of safety and comfort second to none."

The design is clean, crisp, futuristic, and comfortable. It does not interfere with hats, bike helmets, hoodies, or any type of earrings. It repels sweat, dust, and moisture.

The state of California passed a law that prohibits riding a bicycle and wearing headphones that cover both of your ears, because that may prevent a rider from remaining aware of his surroundings. France has a law which states that you're not allowed to wear headphones while you're driving, riding a bike or riding your scooter. Our product provided for situational awareness with both ears uncovered.

We had to determine what kind of competitors we were going to be up against in this new market, Direct, which means the competitor would be producing the same or a highly similar product, or Indirect, which products might provide a portion of what our product could deliver, but the price differential for a lesser functioning product, might be sufficient to take the sale from us.

We would also have to carefully evaluate our competitor's strengths and weaknesses, determine who their customer base was, the age group, gender appeal, and how the end-user envisioned product use. For what use and why was the product purchase being considered?

We would also have to review internet search terms a potential purchaser might use to describe the type of product being sought by a potential purchaser. Might the product benefit from being advertised under multiple descriptions? For example, should we also consider listing it under Bluetooth® compatible smartphone earphones with an eye toward presenting a superior product in a viable price range for a shopper? Our competitor had not done so. Did they overlook the marketing potential of that category? Or have they already tried it without success?

There are myriad questions which will need to be answered during your research of any product. Look deep. The more homework you do, the more you understand your competitor, the greater the market share you're likely to capture.

A word to the wise is sufficient!

Passion is contagious.
So is complacency.

Chapter 4

Passion Play

Chapter 4

Passion Play

You can't expect others to buy in to what you are selling if you are not passionate about it yourself. *"Science says passion is contagious,"* wrote Carmine Gallo. But so is complacency.

It has been said that winning is everything. What do *you* say? Without passion, we will not win. Critical to winning is passion. If winning is all important to you, then you need to prove it, by being on time (albeit 15 minutes early) and, you need to prove it by thinking ahead, anticipating not just those things and events that are expected to happen, but things which may be beyond your control. You need to have a back-up plan in place. You need to continually seek to improve not only the system, but its people.

It is a tough assignment to commit to a cause, or to being involved in development of a new product, but both happen at the same time – result? A passion for a product or service to be sold to a waiting, yearning, often breathless consumer, who anticipates that he or she will get every single thing that you talked about, and expects to receive all of them easily, and with no flaws.

Never happens. One of the first things that can go wrong is that the initial on-time delivery doesn't show up as promised. Sometimes that's the fault of Mother Nature. Hurricanes, tornados, major storms, hail, unexpected floods, wildfires, related road closures, and airport delays, are all possible problems, but more often it's a postal or delivery service error. Some problems are to be anticipated but, some remain mysteries to be uncovered only after finding a real live person with at least a modicum of awareness of the problem's existence.

In the meantime, the unhappy, unsatisfied consumer is writing angry, negative reviews online, defining the various failures as the fault of the seller, ignoring all of the related hold-up events. This is an era, especially in the digital age, in which unhappy customers can do serious damage to a company with a single click of a mouse. In the past, a disgruntled customer who was dissatisfied with a company's customer-service, would likely call the Better Business Bureau, who in turn would call a supervisor at the seller's facility, formally bring the matter to the company's attention, then ride herd until the matter was resolved amicably, and to the satisfaction of all parties. The complaint would be marked resolved and everybody would be happy. Today there are online review sites such as Yelp, which allow users to post angry reviews, ascribe a 1 to 5 star rating and spitefully issue a 1-star rating to tangibly express their annoyance. There are multiple problems with this system. First and foremost, the seller is literally not permitted to respond to the posted complaint. There have also been instances where an angry customer has posted a scathing review on a page belonging to a totally innocent company, often one which had the misfortune to have a vaguely similar name, or occasionally one which simply manufactured a similar product and the angry customer was confused about the product brand he was complaining about. Regardless, in the overwhelming majority of cases, Yelp® flatly refuses to remove negative postings, and will not permit a seller to explain the circumstances in order to rebut the negative review. Were Yelp an obscure review site, that would be one thing, but it's not, thus the link with the reputation damaging review often appears on the first page of a prospective client or end-user's company search.

Yelp itself is widely considered to have abysmal customer service as a result, when in reality, their own telephone answering personnel may be hampered in solving problems, because that's not their job. The review website was only designed to attract advertising. It achieves no revenue from problem resolution. Flaming reviews draw traffic, which in turn, boost the site's ad revenue. There is no motivation to remove negative posts. It's like the Wild West. There's no sheriff around to patrol the streets or protect the innocent, and life is not fair.

Problems often rapidly accelerate in frequency due to a seller's use of untrained and limited-skill workers at the telephone answering end. One major problem a company may experience is with off-shore, non-native English speakers, who are limited to a canned speech, have no actual knowledge of the product itself, or who haltingly read from a general or (worse) a legalese-laden script, rather than actually responding with some level of actual assistance.

We do recall that "CUSTOMER SERVICE" (once upon a time), stood for trying to aid a suffering customer to select the best product for an application; teaching them how to use it if they needed help, figuring out how they could cope in the interim with the vagaries of a delivery-system that tried to meet the needs of the seller, and the realities of a user experiencing delivery service problems. This is a long way of describing an internet-based economy which, in too many cases, neither understands nor cares about the product, its use, delivery problems, or their resolution.

Whatever happened to the routine that included the sending of a personal note from a customer service person directed to a customer, which made both parties feel as if someone cared, or the technique of provision of a customer service representative's phone numbers and email address? These are actions that show that an actual human can be reached by a customer who may simply have wanted to vent and to describe a complaint. This level of service still exists, but it's no longer the rule. Far too often, it's the exception.

The result of a highly charged system that is solely measured by dollars and cents falls short of one which delivers real solutions to real problems. Imagine taking real action(s) while at the same time not blaming anybody else for problems that are rightfully those of the seller. We need to be passionate from the beginning, from description accuracy to delivery, to product usability. Imagine a situation where truth is volunteered every step along the way.

I have personally taken packages to the post office. Now I know (from experience) that Monday is a terrible day to try and get a package shipped. It is a busy time and the system is badly overloaded, whereas later in the week, it is a lot easier when waited upon by a non-rushed, non-abused, well-trained clerk.

Fed Ex® and UPS® both use (running as fast as they are able) drivers that mostly deliver to real people, but are so time constrained, that unless a signature is mandated, will simply leave packages at the door instead of at least taking the time to knock before heading back to the truck, thereby alerting the occupant that someone was, or had just been there. These left packages are readily seen as invitations for theft and, are once again reflected in a need for follow-up to try and locate the missing package. Delivery personnel, whether they're from Fedex, UPS, or local florist delivery drivers who simply leave a box of delicate fresh flowers on a sun-baked, rain soaked, or frozen porch, still don't seem to have learned that simple lesson. Who gets blamed?

You know the truth in all of this. How do you know? Why do you know? It is because you have had the same problems, and since there is little or no way to address the difficulty, problem or error, poor customer service is tolerated.

A truly passionate person feels responsible for every single problem that happens. He or she refuses to be dominated by a system or individual who wants to stay above or beyond the fray. Their passion reaches out to, and is felt by the consumer, and once it becomes clear that it is a sincere effort to help, friendship takes over and the problem either gets solved or something else happens, but the end result is that the customer is not only satisfied, but has become a customer for life. The customer service representative also has a feeling of "I did a good thing."

It takes very little thought and pre-planning to get significant results. It takes a passionate belief in the item or product to be sold, a passionate belief in the company, and most importantly, a passionate care about one's own self.

Passion includes using the customer's name three times at the counter or on the phone. Passion takes listening to the customer's rant about the failures that sparked his or her outrage up to this point. The simple art of sincere and patient listening, of kindness and concern, and being supportive as a result of the listening, really does count. It results in a near flabbergasted customer, one who is amazed that a seller actually cares, speaks clearly, listens, expresses understanding, and furnishes a realistic resolution, or at the least a path leading toward resolution.

Frustration prevails when the system or a component part of the system fails. It is critical (and very difficult to do) to introduce a passion to resolve problems to individuals asked to commit and become involved in an old fashioned idea of care and problem solving. That is especially the case in an environment of greed, with results that are measured not by care, but by the number of phone calls which can be handled by a single operator in one shift. It means that the entire organization, from warehouse to manufacturing plant to sub and final assembly, inspection, marketing and merchandising to the decision makers – all must be passionate about serving the customer.

Sex, Politics, and Religion.
Don't Talk About Them.
Seriously. Don't Do It.

Chapter 5

Politics and Sales Make a Bad Cocktail

Chapter 5

Politics and Sales Make a Bad Cocktail

In the early days of my career, it was easy to keep these two (Politics and Sales) separate. You just wouldn't interject politics into your conversations with clients. Today, social media and real-time, non-stop news reporting, has made keeping the two separate much more difficult.

I'm not encouraging, nor am I asking you to give up your principles and beliefs, rather, I just want you to recognize that if you and your client are on opposite ends of the political spectrum – and they know it - you're going to want to proceed with caution!

Unlike today's political standards, truth turns out to be critically valuable to beginning, maintaining, and to enhancing working relationships. It is necessary to build a strong and lasting friendship with the client you will be dealing with.

There can still be a significant difference in your and your client's view of local and national politics, but there must be trust and honesty between you on a business level. He or she has to feel that the two of you both deal from the top of the deck. No sleight of hand!

In the rare instance where you discover that there is an apparently insurmountable barrier to frank and open (and honest) informational transfer, there are two selections of approach and implementation that must be made for your success in making a presentation.

Choice One is for you to present only salient facts (with any and all needed caveats) which make clear that differing political views are not involved in any part of the step by step process that follows any new sale. The issue is convincing your client that this is both sincere and at the same time serious.

Not only is this a narrow area upon which to tread but it is required as a test of the relationship that you have established with the client. Understanding that your friendship could be at risk in the current political climate may well make your presentation unusually difficult to develop. Also, getting your client both involved and committed to the proposed arrangement can be challenging when there is a significant political and or attitudinal variance between your views, and those of your client. That means you have to tread lightly.

This is the one area in which even generalized discussions can be difficult, and a misjudged attempt at levity can have disastrous potential – so use both caution and care. Do not regard this as casual suggestion. It is important.

The second choice is also fraught with risk. If you find it hard to separate "business-thinking" and (for example) the current levels of tribalism, it may well be wise to either bring to the meeting (or to have on standby for a phone call), a non-threatening individual, whose role is to deal with (for instance), technical matters that do not require your client to bring up, or discuss the things that separate the two of you. Supporting friendship, either a new friendship or one that is seasoned by time, is key.

You have a specific goal in mind; to establish or maintain a relationship with a client. Based on prior conversations leading up to arranging this meeting, you suspect that there may be strong political differences. When you select that "non-threatening" individual, you'll want to verify that this is actually the case. If you're in the middle of a promising discussion, and offer to call an associate who you explain will have the answer to exactly the question just posed by the client during your meeting, you'll want to make sure that you keep the phone conversation short and on track. If the client makes a joke or an inappropriate comment that offends your "non-threatening" individual, you don't want to be sitting there defenseless should that individual instinctively and unexpectedly fire back at the client.

Prep your phone contact, tell him/her you want to discuss only technical or other specifics of the product or production schedule, and warn them not to stray into any other territory. That may help keep the meeting on business rather than politics. Imagine that you are introducing the client to a new design for something that he or she has acquired from you and, has been happy with it in its earlier form.

Your chore is to have fully understood and be able to clearly explain that the advantages of your company's product will create more or better margins for your clients own organization. You will want to stress that the item is less costly or easier to understand, or requires less maintenance, etc. This change of product conversation can be sufficiently all-consuming to minimize whatever the differences in philosophical thought might be.

Evaluation of the differences is just one more complexity that you have to add to your understanding of the client you hope to begin, or continue to serve. It is not a minimalist thing. It is a vital part of the assessment that you are responsible for.

Do not let this deter you. Identify that it is empowering and in many cases puts you on a slightly different course of activity that is both appealing and engaging, without your being boorish. Caution has to be your watchword. Take careful steps, even if you totally agree with your client. Never forget that he or she may well not be in agreement with his or her top management.

Speaking of which, top management can also inadvertently pose a significant problem for sales personnel. Whatever they decide to say or do of a political nature also has the potential to affect every single member of the marketing staff.

For example, company endorsement of a political candidate can be like crossing a minefield blindfolded. It's a journey senior management may not wish to make. Not only will you definitely alienate part of your workforce, you also risk alienating existing and potential clients, and quite possibly the end users of your product, which further negatively affects your company's client.

I'll give you a particularly sobering example. The well-thought-of grocery chain Publix®, headquartered in Lakeland, Florida, has 1,231 stores located throughout the southern states, and employs 193,000 people. The company has an excellent reputation for clean stores, well paying jobs, great customer service, a long history of generous philanthropy, and it offers jobs, dignity, and respect to the differently-abled.

A few years back, in 2012, the company decided to endorse and financially donate to the campaign of a particularly divisive political candidate. Business silently dropped off and their candidate lost. But management either didn't pay attention, or didn't connect the dots.

In 2018 they stepped in it again. On February 14, 2018, a gunman opened fire at Marjory Stoneman Douglas High School in Parkland, Florida, killing seventeen students and staff members, and injuring seventeen others. Three months after the massacre of those children, Publix formally announced the company's support for a Florida gubernatorial candidate backed by the NRA® (National Rifle Association.)

Activist students who survived the horrific massacre and watched friends and teachers die right in front of them, staged a "die-in" at the grocery store, and urged advocates of gun reform (semi-automatic weapons) to stop shopping at Publix until the company withdrew its support for the gubernatorial candidate who had earned a top rating from the powerful gun-rights group, and even once described himself on Twitter as a "proud NRA sellout."

Floridians were outraged by the company's staggering insensitivity. Negative publicity went national and sales took a nosedive. All those good deeds, wiped out in a single, astoundingly tone-deaf decision to support another widely reviled political candidate. The decision was immediately followed by the corporation's frantic back-peddling. "We regret that our contributions have led to a divide in our community. We did not intend to put our associates and the customers they serve in the middle of a political debate," the company said in a statement. Publix management added: "We would never knowingly disappoint our customers or the communities we serve. As a result, we decided earlier this week to suspend corporate-funded political contributions as we reevaluate our giving processes."

Speaking of management, (and *to* management) the job of juggling a workforce comprised of individuals with diametrically opposed political views can be challenging, to say the least. More often it's absolutely daunting. The point of the exercise is to have a smooth-running organization and avoid having a work environment which could, at the drop of a hat, devolve into a shouting match on the factory floor. You're going to have to declare the workplace a neutral zone. And based on the Publix debacle, that lesson should be taken to heart by management as well. And frankly, this is not a bad thing.

And that brings us to hats. And t-shirts. And political buttons.

Take a deep breath and write a company-wide memo. Just do it.

In it consider saying something like this; "While the company respects everyone's individual philosophies and political opinions, they don't belong in the workplace. This company is a team, and we're all on the same side here.

We'd prefer that you left your strongly held philosophical views at home. Seriously. Whatever it is, if it's divisive, it doesn't belong here. If that slogan hat or coffee mug is the only one you own, we'll be happy to give you one with our company logo on it instead.

If your t-shirt blares a political message, regardless of whether it's a polite, or an in-your-face comment, we have a stack of company logo t-shirts, and there's probably one in that pile that will fit you.

Here's our take on the state of affairs; Our hiring policies are gender neutral and the pay rate is based on the job, not the gender or color, or faith, or nationality or political affiliation of the person selected to serve in that position. Character counts, and we believe that honesty is the best policy. We're open to constructive criticism, and we value good ideas. We have one goal here, and that's to make this company a success, and in doing so, provide a good paying job for each of our employees."

Kate Headley, principal consultant at a PR firm in Ottowa, Canada summed it up rather nicely. "Before making a public political statement, a company needs to have an honest internal conversation about what statement they're making, the real reasons behind it, and what they hope to achieve. There's no such thing as a political issue where 100 per cent of people agree with each other. When assessing whether or not to take a stance, a company first needs to consider how it will affect their primary stakeholders, customers, investors and staff."

Food for thought.

Telephones 101

Chapter 6

Make Your Own Phone Calls

Chapter 6

Make Your Own Phone Calls

Although the practice has been around for a very long time, particularly in large corporations, I've always thought it incredibly pretentious to have an assistant call me and then have them say "*Please hold while I connect you to Mr. Big.*"

I once had a recruiter try and sell me his placement software. He had one of his admin call to tell me to go to a particular website where I could set up a call with him when he was available. *Really?* I'm running a business, you're trying to sell me something, and I'm supposed to go to *your* website, check *your* availability and then *I'm* supposed to schedule a time for *me* to call *you*, at *your* convenience? *Seriously?*

I get it. That caller was a busy guy but still, he wanted to make a sale. Instead, all he managed to do with that call was negatively affect the likelihood that I would consider accepting his future calls. He successfully turned me off as a potential buyer. He made a poor impression by putting his need to prospect for a sale, over whatever my busy schedule happened to be that day. He let me know that he didn't care about me or my company's needs, only about his personal desire to make a sale. And, to top it all off, I considered the manner in which it was done to be unprofessional.

So no, I didn't make that call and, more importantly, I didn't buy anything from him. Here's my take on that situation. When you want to get something done, it's *your* responsibility to see that it happens, and not the other way around. First of all, you need to respect your prospective purchaser. My caller didn't do that.

Unless you're scheduling a multi-person conference call, telephoning in advance to set up a second call is not really the way to go. Frankly, it annoys the buyer who is being forced to accept a call he/she doesn't particularly want to be bothered with in the first place. On any given day, there are other matters which need his/her immediate attention.

These days, the sheer deluge of sales calls one receives is frustrating, and it often gets to a point where the mere sound of a telephone ringing actually antagonizes the recipient.

When you put your marketing hat on, the first thing you need to remember is that your potential client is busy. He or she has a business or department to run. You have a product that you believe has the potential to become a desirable asset to his/her business, and, you'd like that company to know about it.

By the way, what makes you think this company would be interested in your product? Is this your first attempt to gain the company's business?

What do you know about that person? What do you know about that company? You'll want to have done your homework before making the call. It's more than likely that you'll need to get past the gatekeeper first when you do call. Marketing calls of one sort or another come in all day long. The better prepared you are to talk your way past a secretary or administrative assistant, the better chance you'll have to reach the buyer personally to gain an in-person appointment to make that sale.

It's the gatekeeper's job to evaluate what you have to say and decide whether to connect that call, take a message, or forget that it ever happened. Many fall into the latter category.

An enormous number of the calls we receive every day are annoying. They fall into the nuisance category.

Among the most annoying calls, of course, are the impersonal robocalls which attempt to trick the call recipient into saying the word "Yes" which is duly recorded, and used as a pretext to ship a subscription to a publication you didn't want, which will then be followed by a bill for receipt of the subscription.

Number two in annoying calls are the ones from offshore boiler-rooms where an individual whose grasp of the English language is tenuous at best, and whose accent is so heavy it's nigh onto impossible to even discern the words comprising the greeting. That's generally followed by the caller haltingly reading from a script. If you interrupt the caller with, "I'm sorry, I'm having difficulty understanding you. Could you please repeat the name of your company?" the caller actually goes back to the very beginning of the script and begins reading it in the same unintelligible dialect.

Again you politely repeat, "I'm sorry, perhaps we have a bad connection. I still don't understand you. Can you spell that name for me, please?" The caller will helpfully spell it, but you won't be able to understand that either, and the caller will once again begin reading the script from the beginning.

The very worst of course, is a similar call with a heavy accent, but one in which the caller identifies himself by a laughably unlikely name. "Good morning, sir. My name is Clint Eastwood, and I am calling to discuss with you my company's product."

So by the time you, as a professional, with a product that is well worthy of a potential client's attention, make your own call, the person on the other end of the line is not particularly inclined to hear much of anything that doesn't make exceptionally good sense.

The last thing you need is a hostile client, or a hostile gatekeeper, for that matter, so if you have made it past the gatekeeper, instead of immediately launching into an extended sales pitch, you'll to want listen carefully for a moment and try to gauge the client's mood. It's a good way to lessen the annoyance factor.

If he sounds relaxed and chatty you have plenty of time. If not, you'll want to give it your best 45 second shot without sounding rushed.

"Thanks for taking a moment to speak with me. I know you're busy, so I'll make this brief... My company is currently supplying the WhizBangg company with furball components to speed production and cut manufacturing costs of their Stainless Steel Widget and Gadget products.

If I understand your own product line correctly, it's possible that our new furball line of components could vastly improve Fooberly's production speed and significantly increase Fooberly's net profit at the same time. We've designed furball components to be fully compatible with a wide range of manufacturing materials, from plastic to Titanium®. Retooling? Bare minimum and the installation expense would be negligible. Could you spare me a few minutes sometime either this week or next so that I can swing by and give you some exact numbers based on your current production figures?"

Structure your pitch to make every one of those 45 seconds count. Do it right, and you have a foot in the door with one phone call.

One of the most important divisions of a company is telephone tech-support. It doesn't matter whether your company employs off-shore tech support or has tech-support situated in-house. It also doesn't matter that you've worked hard to motivate your telephone answering people, and teach them how to handle problems and answer customer questions thoroughly, correctly and clearly to consumers. There are always situations which require a back-up plan.

The occasional questions that telephone customer service employees do not know how to handle. When they're flummoxed or stuck for an answer to a product user, it makes sense to instruct customer service personnel to tell the customer that they wouldn't want to give incorrect or incomplete information, so they want to call in a supervisor to make certain the problem is quickly resolved. If need be, support can tell the customer the supervisor is busy with another customer at the moment but you can promise to call them back in ten minutes and tell them that when you do, you'll stay with them until the supervisor is on the line.

This step identifies the customer as important. It also shows that the individual responding to his or her question has flagged the matter as being of immediate importance.

Hopefully, the unhappy consumer by now realizes that their concern will be quickly and properly addressed.

Your phone support team needs to understand that it's imperative to get that caller to the person who knows the most about either the matter at hand, or the specific device with which they are having a problem. You want your phone support team member to know who they can depend on in this situation. Who knows the most *about* this situation? That list should be right in front of them.

Obtain critical information from the caller so the right expert can be called in. That way the understanding of the problem can be confirmed by the supervisor without the need for clients to go through the aggravating process of repeating the complaint a second time, since that will only further upset them. This also reinforces the caller's decision to have purchased your company's product in the first place. It also goes a long way toward buyer retention for that next purchase.

Once that call has ended the team member can attempt to quickly resolve the problem with the help of the designated supervisor. If it cannot be done without having the customer on the line the customer call-back *must* be made within the promised time frame.

Some customers expand the relationship with the telephone customer service person too far. They might just want to chat. Sometimes this is something that needs to be controlled to protect both the customer and the company. "Time to get both of us back to work isn't it?" Every once in a while a customer carries it too far. They go beyond. A great manager can help.

The customer is "always right". Except when the only alternative to unending discussions, becomes determining how or what is necessary to resolve an issue. This is the point where turning the customer over to the area manager so the customer can speak directly to him (or her) is the best alternative.

A good natured manager can only try and view the problem in the same way the customer does. This translates into letting the customer vent his or her difficulties. All a manager can do is assure the customer that he/she will devote whatever time it takes and will do his/her very best to get the situation clarified and resolved to the customer's satisfaction.

The possibility exists, of course, that the problem might ultimately not be capable of being corrected. The manager will listen carefully however, letting the customer be heard and permitting the complaint situation to be outlined in detail. Then the manager can assist.

At the very heart of handling unhappy customers, there is always a reminder that all of the problems started with the customer's initial expectations of a high quality product delivered, or available for pick-up in-store and on-time, available at a fair price, and that the product will be usable exactly as its advertising or sales document promised.

Customer service is there to assist and to explain what can be explained, and personnel have been provided with tools, which, properly used, have been designed to make the customer happy. That's the objective!

As a marketing specialist, it is *your* job to figure out *how* your Widget is used, as well as how it could be *improved*. You are ultimately responsible for how and where your product is shelved in outlets, and how it is to benefit consumers as it is used. It's your responsibility to make it a better understood Widget and, at the same time to have its purchase increased, the desired end result being that users feel good about the Widget's selection, and their ultimate purchase.

The most important lesson which can be taken away from our various telephone interactions is that proper use of that single tool, one of many at our disposal, offers an opportunity to either generate (or lose) business, add a personal touch to client and associate interactions, stay up-to date with what's happening in our own company and get a feel for real customers.

Back in 1989, during a walk-through inspection of a new customer service facility, billionaire Bill Gates impulsively grabbed a headset, sat down at a desk and took an incoming call. "Hello, this is Microsoft Product Support, William speaking. How can I help you?" Gates searched the product database, walked the customer through the problem-solving routine, and closed with "Thank you for using Microsoft products." A little bit later that day the customer called back with a different question, and asked to again be connected to that "nice man named William who straightened it all out."

William made a very good impression.

Clients prefer to do business with people they like, and those they can identify with.

Chapter 7

The Chameleon Effect

Chapter 7

The Chameleon Effect

It's said the profession of sales is somewhat akin to being a psychologist. That's at least partially true. For example, I was recently reading a Shopify® blog, and came across the book entitled "Presuasion" by Robert Cialdini. In it, he addresses seven of the principles of the psychology of selling.

Among those principles are "Liking" and "Sameness" (i.e. identification with each other) and points out that people find it much easier to live and work among those they identify with or with whom they easily find common ground.

An interesting example took place during World War II when in the late 1930's the Japanese were accepting displaced Jews into their country. In 1942, however, when Emperor Hirohito of Japan chose to ally his country with the other two Axis powers, led by Adolf Hitler of Germany, and Benito Mussolini of Italy, the country of Japan found itself under pressure from Germany to get rid of the Jews. When members of the Japanese High Command met with Jewish leaders, they asked "Why do the Germans hate you so much?" It was Rabbi Kalisch who replied, "Because we are Asians – like you." With this single statement, the concept of "sameness" was established, and Japan chose to protect its Jewish community. The lives of thousands were spared.

When it comes to business, picking up on the personality traits of an individual will allow you to establish your approach while also adjusting to another individual's non-verbal signals and traits.

We like people who are similar to us, we like people who pay us compliments, and we like people who cooperate with us towards mutual goals.

Like the chameleon, you can adjust your "selling colors" to suit the particular atmosphere or environment you have found yourself in. At the same time, just like the chameleon which changes its color to blend in with the environment in which it finds itself, you'll find that you can appear to agree with various positions yet still be you.

Yes, it's complex. It does require your being super-observant and to consciously try and temporarily adapt to another's environment. You can do this. You do it normally with those people you have a special interest in. For example: you may consciously or subconsciously adapt to meet the personality of someone who is louder and more demonstrative than you are normally. Or, the reverse may be the choice. That is to say, adapt to being quiet, reticent and self-deprecating. It is not difficult and it is not something that should be avoided because you think it might be considered "phony." It is a natural attribute that some people have, but most don't.

The chameleon ability can not only be learned, it can be learned without causing problems.

Regional accents are something that humans often find themselves mimicking. Drop somebody from the Midwest into a group from the "deep South" for a while and in no time at all, the word "Ya'll" and a soft twang are likely to become part of the Midwesterner's vocabulary. They are unconsciously demonstrating chameleon-like traits which allow them to better blend in with their new surroundings.

To develop adaptability requires only that you listen and listen carefully to the other person's views, while thinking positively about the individual you are with. What are his or her best qualities? What makes him or her happiest? If he is in favor of a particular sport, a team or an individual, and even if you disagree with the choices, there is a bond that can be developed which can be of real import when the negotiation is changed to discussing a sales item.

For example, consider if the individual with whom you need to have a good working relationship, unwisely brings up politics in the highly polarized environment in which we currently find ourselves. In this type of business atmosphere, for you to give even a glimpse of either support or denial of any given political stance is intuitively forbidden by the very logic you employed to acquire this book. In the words of the fictional Michael Corleone from *The Godfather*, "It's not personal, Sonny. It's strictly business."

This is the time for you to listen and politely abstain from remarking on politics. A good way of doing that would to smile pleasantly and say "I make it a point never to mix business and politics, however I suspect that you and I share a number of similar philosophies," and leave it at that. It's likely truthful. You both probably like Golden Retrievers, cats, and fishing.

Should the conversation continue unabated, you can simply smile slightly, while nodding or shaking your head imperceptibly, as if agreeing or disagreeing. Even if you strongly disagree, this is the time to grit your teeth and feign support. This is the chance and the time to build a strong friendship and the very time (if it helps), to recognize that this is the action that may eventually rebuild American bilateral solidarity.

It is not easy, nor is it "faking." It is adapting without exposing your individual (constitution-given and guaranteed) right to an opinion, even if it's contrary to that of your customer. After all, you have no idea if his or her company owners have any firm convictions one way or another. On the other hand, it's quite possible that the only real deal-killer would be if the other company itself held and publicized extremist positions which either espoused hate or supported the denial of equal rights under the constitution, in which case, you'd hardly be faulted for promptly departing.

Forgetting that (hopefully) unlikely condition, your role is simply to be supportive, without the need to agree with views different from either your own, or those held by your company's leaders. Instead your tactic will rely upon being polite and diplomatic instead of dramatically shaking your head, rolling your eyes, and wondering out loud if the other party is insane.

Yes, it is sort of akin to functioning as an undercover agent. You temporarily adapt your persona to accommodate your prospect's stance, often murmuring a noncommittal *"mmmm"* in perceived agreement. Accommodate, not as you, only as a polite and thoughtful supporter of the person who was unwise enough to bring up a political or politically-charged issue without having the intellectual foresight to first take the measure of the room.

The chameleon changes color as it is required to, but without giving up its individuality. You can blend in without giving up your support of a competing vision which differs significantly from the viewpoint of another.

The role is not simple nor is it readily definable. It means that you assess not only what your potential prospect feels, but it means that you have a mature view of your own support system as it relates to politics. You may well find other areas of agreement that you can bond over, such as the need to do something about the toxic algae choking our waterways and destroying once pristine fishing grounds.

We defined this as a complex area and it is. To ignore my counsel on this is to ignore the realities that happen on a daily, in fact, minute by minute basis. Keeping your feet squarely on the ground while all about you, there are leaders, prospects and consumers whose ideas and positions differ sharply from your own is not just desirable, it is mandatory. This has always been the case.

The value in constantly displaying a clearly stated position is not nearly as important as it used to be. The advent of constant news information joined with social media, coupled with voter importance, coupled with voter non-involvement, has made it acceptable to ignore nearly all of the information given out by politicians, talking heads, and the written word. You become unique because, as a sales maven, you have the best opportunity to hear how a position exists in, from, or for your prospect, without jeopardizing your own views.

The most successful marketers and sales people are able to go from supporter to disagreement on just about any subject in a split second. You can too. Or not. It depends on your level of maturity, and perhaps your ability to play poker.

You're playing for money here.

Chapter 8

Patience Is A Virtue

Chapter 8

Patience Is A Virtue

Patience is important. Time, we understand <u>heals all wounds</u> and, as one of its palliative qualities, is that it <u>wounds all heels</u>. Applying patience to meeting demands of clients sets us apart from those who irritate clients by transferring them to others who may have even less problem-solving capabilities. Naturally, a worse alternative is to respond with a less than empathetic response which subtly suggests "we make crappy products, deal with it," instead of having a fully trained, clear-speaking individual tell the client "*I am so sorry about that. It is most disappointing. Perhaps we had a slight mistake in manufacturing or possibly it suffered shipping damage. We'll be happy to exchange it. May I send you a replacement right away?*"

It is pointed out that while this is a long answer to a short request, the client had three important objectives which were met. It sympathizes with the client's frustrating experience; it explains what the problem might have been and, it offers a clear and immediate solution.

Depending on what was being sold, it may have been appropriate to state, "*Or, should I send you a complete refund?*" In either case, the client was to be satisfied and, the client was treated with care.

That is the specific objective of all support furnished.

If an item is not available, it is never easy to tell a client that a specific item isn't available now. It happens to be backordered but will be available next month. There are two possible answers to be given, and the psychology of phrasing your answer is important:

1) *I can't send you that item until next month. It's backordered and unavailable now.* Or,

2) *It will be available next month, I can place an order right now for you and then make certain it gets sent to your address as quickly as it reaches our warehouse.*

The first answer is almost certain to elicit an angry answer from the client whereas, the second puts emphasis on what the client actually cares about and thus makes the client happy. The client is the concern. The second reply as a positive answer, gave the client reasons to be reasonably content and to keep him or her from going to our competitor for a similar, but inferior item.

It would be remiss to not digress to a telephone request when an operator says

"*Please hold while we transfer your call. Your call is very important to us.*" And then after a protracted delay, a different voice comes on telling me "*your call is very important to us"* then, this vitally important call slides into a commercial for a product, then some music and yet another voice to tell me how valuable this call is to them. If I am still on the phone it is because it is urgent or because I have fallen asleep.

Even worse is when the voice tells me "*I am sorry, but I'm going to have to transfer your call to department X.*" By now I am annoyed and feeling ignored. I'm getting passed around like a leftover cookie, and I am now irate enough to just about choke someone. I haven't once been able to speak to a single human being beyond the initial operator who answered. And, I have been hanging on long enough that my phone's battery is running down.

When a client has been terribly treated, both with failure to deliver followed by an additional telephone blow, the client can be angry. Sometimes the anger is unjustified, but oftentimes it isn't. It's a tough problem, that of wooing a seriously disgruntled client from the brink or possibly even farther out.

There is no perfect solution but there are four steps which apply and are meaningful to clients who are outraged at your company.

Sincere apology helps. You are the point person hence you are required to take the brunt of the blame. So, saying you are sorry is as good as it gets for a starting place.

Angry clients want sympathy. They want your emphatic support of their state of madness. Walk a mile in their shoes and understand why the client is so angry. This is business, where sometimes things do not progress the way they were originally anticipated to proceed. Acknowledge their concern and try to get them to see that you are taking the blame for a failure, and that you feel the same pangs he or she does.

Your willingness to accept responsibility for a problem reflects your company's attitudes about the way your company affects your client personally and their organization directly. It is the bottom line. And, the bottom point. Now that you have melded feelings, their organization has to feel that a pound of flesh has been ripped from your aching bones. This is the chance to have you make it right and fix it for the client.

The real terms and conditions for fixing the problem include having a certain delivery date for resolution and, making certain that there is a viable solution for the underlying issue that caused the difficulty in the first place.

If it was actually the client that pushed for an unrealistic delivery date, or a device feature that has turned out to be really difficult – it is more than a usual issue problem. If the client had asked and someone responded "*no-sweat we can do it*" but was wrong, then deliberately hid the issue by not announcing that there actually was a problem, the issue blossoms into a major headache for all concerned. Happens? Yep.

Delivery is not nearly as difficult the second time around. But, what *is* hard is resolution of the emotional issue that riled up the client. This is where you get to use all your skills to both be contrite when it comes to admitting guilt and at the same time calm the client down and convince him enough so he can leave both mollified and happy. This takes both time and patience. It takes solving problems and working with people. If you are successful, then you've done a NICE JOB.

If he is still upset and remains unimpressed with your wisdom, demeanor and apologetic words, then recognize that there is nothing else that could have been done. There are always situations that simply cannot be resolved, because the client doesn't really want them to be resolved. The client simply wanted someone to argue with. At least you gave it your best try.

The ultimate compliment
from a customer is to be
considered an advocate
for their business.

Chapter 9

The Benefits of Advocacy

Chapter 9

The Benefits of Advocacy

Advocacy Marketing is a form of marketing that emphasizes getting existing customers to talk about the company and its products. More than 80% of shoppers research a product online before buying. BigCommerce®

Four out of five consumers have changed their minds about buying a product or service, based on negative online information. INC. ®

Regardless of what your last purchase was, from flip-flops to flat screens, odds are that you went online, searched for the product, read reviews, compared identical and similar products made by different manufacturers, checked out brands, models, reliability scores, evaluated pros and cons, and paid attention to customer service reports.

Next you evaluated whether to purchase the product locally or have it shipped to you. You checked local prices, you checked shipping. You weighed instant gratification against saving a few bucks.

The same thing holds true for manufacturer sales reps when it comes to product lines they'd *prefer* to represent, but it's especially true for retailers when determining which products they want to stock for their customers. They don't need customer complaint headaches any more than you do. Today 8 out of 10 people have developed a habit of doing their homework before making a commitment. And today that goes for everything from buying a house to choosing a mate.

Your clients depend upon you to provide them with reliable products, delivered as promised, and as close to headache-free as possible.

The ultimate compliment is for you, as a professional, to be considered an advocate for your client's business. That doesn't happen overnight, but is to be developed over time, and has as its goal a functioning, continuing working relationship.

It shows that you are trusted. It is a most serious business when you become trusted as a supplier; trusted to bring to the client products and even ideas that will be of benefit to your client. And, it also means that the products and ideas you bring will get a look and examination by and from that client, rather than an offhand brush-off. That brush-off is typical for products or ideas that are offered without support, or are brought to the table too early in a relationship, without having the seasoning which only comes from both a serious and successful, longer term relationship.

Initially trust begins to be created by your "coming across" a magazine article, or a blog or a social media post or the like that you bring to them, thereby showing that you care for, and about their business. Simple, carefully programmed steps, can demonstrate that you're thinking of them, and that you have their best interests at heart.

In my career, I worked hard to develop trust, to the point where I had a client tell me to just go ahead and write the order for them. By making their jobs easier and more productive, while recognizing and respecting their time, you're doing things on their behalf, and they show their appreciation in differing ways. Additional business is the goal.

I would love to be able to report that in every single instance the client fully and openly expresses their thanks. It is not that way. There are clients that want to take all the credit for a success, and others who view your help as a threat to them and their business aspirations. Then there are also those who have so much pressure on them that they literally don't have the time to consider alternative methods or products; even those that could free them up.

Not openly recognizing their reliance on your constant help is all part of the business. Nonetheless, there will come a time when your assistance is both needed as well as wanted. That day *does* always come. Now this is important; it's paramount for you to realize that *you must not gloat* when it happens. Treat it like a normal part of the business. You're simply happy to help. Treating the situation that way will help you begin to establish a special relationship with your client. You're all about doing what's going to help your client succeed.

Keep track of what you do to help your client. It's what separates you from somebody trying to take that account away from your company. List the big things and all of the little things you do and tuck them in the file, because one of these days that list is likely to help you retain that account. You can use them to demonstrate part of the service that you have already demonstrated you render to your client. It *is* the major difference which separates you from your competitors.

Advocacy has important and continuing benefits, but not everyone trumpets their satisfaction with your services and their admiration for your products. But be aware that many if not all your clients discuss your capabilities as a supplier-albeit under controlled circumstances, because of Federal, State or local non-competition requirements.

The product price and benefits you offer to your client may not always be outstanding, and in many cases, you may not even have the lowest bid, but you might still get the order. That's because you make it a habit to go above and beyond for your client. You continually strive for leadership in the customer service role. And that's why you're the one they do business with.

Separating the enthusiastic amateur from the sales professional is the difference between what you should expect from every call made on all clients and on all organizations that are not as yet your clients. Remember, the not-yet client category is the future. It is when the fact that you're a great salesperson versus a mere normal or good practitioner of the selling art, makes that all-important difference. It determines your company's growth, and along with taking care of the client, it cements your future in your company.

As our presence in the digital age becomes more pronounced we're noticing more than ever the benefits of advocacy. We're also noticing blatant attempts to cheat by paying for fake reviews.

eBay® experienced some of the first of this problem. Buyers trust Sellers with 100% positive feedback. Unfortunately eBay made no distinction between buying and selling when tallying feedback response. For example if you sold a widget for $100 and received a positive review from your buyer, you would receive 1 positive credit toward your feedback rating. If you *bought* a widget for twenty cents and gave the seller a positive review, you would *also* get 1 more credit towards your positive feedback rating. Gaming the feedback rating system was hardly brain surgery. Practically overnight some sellers were displaying positive feedback ratings in the thousands.

Veteran buyers now look at negative feedback, typically a tiny fraction of the positive feedback rating, but the accompanying comments tell the real story.

Amazon, the 800 pound gorilla in the online marketing room, allowed the practice of incentivized reviews to exist for two decades. Reviewers simply had to disclose the fact that they had received a free or discounted product, in return for the review. What started out as a brilliant idea by Jeff Bezos *"Consumers make smarter choices shopping online than in brick-and-mortar stores because tech platforms enable them to instantly access the opinions of fellow shoppers"* rapidly went south.

It took Amazon until 2015 to begin to crack down on what was finally identified as having become a significant problem. Amazon says it uses artificial intelligence to analyze "hundreds of thousands" of Amazon customers who have now been banned from leaving reviews, and uses the data collected to build computer models of their behavior to predict future techniques."

But Murphy's Law interceded, and when the software targeted their book sales division, the solution amounted to using a shotgun on a mouse. They targeted books by independent authors.

Amazon's software compared an author's friends, relatives, business associates, *and* their Facebook® "friend" list to those book buyers who bought the book, and if they liked it, took the time to leave a positive review for the author's book. Amazon® then cheerfully *deleted* thousands upon thousands of perfectly valid reviews, placed by any names that *matched* the poor author's friends, relatives, business associates, *and* their Facebook "friend" list. Howls of outrage and indignation followed. The complaints fell on deaf ears.

Fake review problems have persisted, of course. Actually they've exploded. So much so that the Washington Post® recently published a large article in which it featured the distress of legitimate sellers who bemoaned the problem but had no idea what to do about it. WaPo® found that some popular product categories were particularly vulnerable to fake reviews, among them Bluetooth® headphones and Bluetooth speakers. Between 50% and 60% of the reviews were discovered to be fake. Of the 47,846 total reviews for the first 10 products listed in an Amazon search for "Bluetooth speakers," *two-thirds* were problematic.

The flood of fake reviews can crush profits. For example, the owner of a baby-products company described the problem as "devastating." Over the past year and a half, he said, his product ratings have plummeted, and he attributes it to a tsunami of fake reviews which benefit his competitors. Amazon has filed five lawsuits since 2015 against people who write paid reviews and the companies who hire them.

According to survey data by the digital marketing firm BloomReach® more than half of *all* online product searches start on Amazon. But of course, Amazon is just the tip of the iceberg.

The fake review problem will eventually be solved. Or it won't. Regardless, it's important for you to be aware of it. That's because consumers tend to give greater credence to peer reviews than they do to print ads, paid internet ads, and television commercials.

There's one notable exception to that rule; The EDS® "Herding Cats" marketing campaign. The TV commercial debuted on January 30, 2000 during Super Bowl XXXIV.

Easily 99% of the people who watched the Super Bowl® had absolutely no idea who EDS was, what it did, or for that matter, what the company could do *for* them, but they loved the ad so much that EDS's business benefited and nearly two decades later, the commercial is still considered one of the advertising industry's all time greatest.

The 'Cat Herders' spot ran through 2001 and it was an unqualified success for EDS. The initial investment of about $8-million brought in an *additional $12 million in 'incremental PR" with a whopping 233 outlets mentioning EDS in pre-and-post-Super Bowl coverage. The ad won numerous awards, including an Emmy® Award nomination. Hits to the company's website soared to five times its normal rate, brand awareness increased 40% year on year in 2000. EDS enjoyed an improvement in employee morale and corporate image, along with new contracts and acquisitions. Fourth-quarter earnings were $5.2 billion, a new quarterly high for the company. There was also "an influx of resumes" at the company following the "Cat Herders" commercial airing.**

Although the Cat Herders spot was part of a marketing campaign, the result was the viral equivalent of advocacy marketing.

Almost everyone who saw the commercial told everyone they knew about it, which prompted other people to go online, learn who EDS was, what they did, who their competitors were, and find out whether those services could benefit their own company.

Advocacy marketing. Worth its weight in gold.

*Source: http://marketing-case-studies.blogspot.com/2008/09/cat-herders-campaign.html

The quickest way to destroy
a relationship with a client
is to become argumentative.

Chapter 10

Let's Not Get Pissy

Let's Not Get Pissy

Pissy (Pis-Sy) Adj. *1. Easily irritated or bitter 2. Abnormally sensitive to a stimulus 3. State of being excessively bitchy without due cause 4. Excessive.*

Things are definitely not going well for Fred M. who, after carefully writing out his plans to deal with a major screw-up, is now dealing with the flak, and has begun talking to himself, since it feels like nobody else is talking to him.

XYZ has 172 stores in the state of Florida and they've got a long-planned sale of multi-colored electronic widgets as loss leaders for their statewide holiday sale. There's a full color six-page ad insert that will run in every major newspaper across the entire state. This product is featured on the front page. This is a big deal. Their distribution center ordered these widgets far in advance so as to avoid any possible delivery problem. The ad hits in ten days time. The "door-buster" sale is scheduled to start in twelve days.

A mistake has been made.

Here's something important. *Confirm* that you've actually made a mistake *before* you admit to it. Did you forget that you immediately advised the client there was going to be a delay? Did you get an OK for an extension? Do you know where those documents are? You always keep paper copies and your computer is backed up. You can find it. Never happened? You really *did* screw up?

Suck it up and admit it, Princess.

The person you're going to be apologizing to is the one whose life, business, and reputation you just screwed up.

You're going to have to fall on your sword.

Trying to dodge responsibility or playing the blame game is only going to make it worse. Much worse. It's also going to make you look like a total jerk. Worst case scenario, the client will take his/her business to another supplier.

Your boss will not be amused, and you'll likely be haunting Monster for a new job. Without glowing references.

So there it is. It's definite. You screwed up. Big time. And it's too late for the client to change their newspaper artwork or reschedule their TV ads. You discovered the screw-up two weeks ago. An integral component was on back-order, you didn't know about it, and it didn't even arrive at your company until a week ago. You notified the client immediately, of course, told them your company was pulling out all stops to try to make the revised delivery deadline, which is day after tomorrow. Which means *they* still have to get it to all of *their* stores, but that's going to mean rush delivery because their fleet of trucks is…*well, you get the picture.* The whole thing is F.U.B.A.R.

You still might be able to pull this one off, but then again, you might not. Naturally you immediately notified your upper management, you begged the new plant manager for a miracle. She's doing her best. She's got the plant running 18-hour shifts, and your company is paying its employees overtime in a valiant attempt to keep from letting your client down.

In the meantime, your client still doesn't know whether your emergency solution is going to fly or not, so they really might be left holding the bag on this one. Your client is not a happy camper. Your CEO is not a happy camper. The crew is dog-tired, and the exhausted plant manager is less than thrilled to be working these hours. Her husband and kids are having frozen pizza for dinner for the fifth night in a row, and you feel like you're silently catching grief from all sides.

YOU know how the screw-up happened, the original plant manager was abruptly discharged. He was eventually replaced by a new plant manager who appears to be very competent, but she was effectively air-dropped into the middle of a war-zone, and she had no idea this order even existed.

Your admin had been instructed to send regular emails to the plant manager to request immediate notification of any potential delays in delivery of the components for your client's order. Of course, the plant manager was no longer with the firm, so his email in-box is currently overflowing with emails. Nobody told the webmaster to route those communications to the new plant manager.

It never occurred to your admin to request affirmative or negative responses to her regular inquiries on job status, she just e-mailed status inquiries out. Nobody told her to expect answers, and the idea apparently never occurred to her, so she would have had no idea anyway that her messages had been consigned to a black hole in cyberspace. Ignorance, apparently, is bliss. You can feel yourself becoming annoyed.

But bottom line, the responsibility was yours, because none of that logical stuff occurred to you either. And by the way, you're the one whose job it was to never have this kind of problem. Which brings us back to our original conclusion; You screwed up. Big time.

When you went to upper management to confess the bad news, you didn't cast blame on the departing plant manager, or the admin, or the webmaster. You shouldered all of the blame yourself. But it's beginning to feel like maybe you should have shared some of that blame.

And frankly, you're feeling a little pissy about it. You know that copping a defensive attitude is not going to win friends and influence people, but still, it's starting to feel like Custer's last stand around here.

Maybe you're imagining it, maybe your co-workers are not looking at you and thinking *"jerk."*

Maybe upper management is not thinking about canning you as soon as this mess is cleaned up.

Maybe the client isn't going to replace your company as a supplier after all. But then again, maybe they are. You're becoming paranoid.

The more all of this simmers in your head, the more defensive your mental attitude is becoming. You've got to get your act together before you actually open your mouth and stick your foot in it. The client is calling at least three times a day to check on status. Your VP is asking for updates at least once an hour. OK, you're exaggerating. But at least once a day.

Take a deep breath. Count to ten. You can do this.

This morning you wanted to snap and yell at the V.P. *"You dope! Don't you think I'd let you know the minute we've got the order packed, and we've called for a pick-up?"* Thankfully, you didn't do that.

Take another deep breath. Count to ten again. You can do this.

Human nature is such that under extreme pressure you might become defensive enough to reach the *pissy* stage when a client complains. Naturally you correctly understand that the fastest way to destroy a relationship with a client is to become argumentative or try to play the blame game in an attempt to absolve yourself of responsibility.

Dealing with a complaining customer is difficult. It represents the ultimate customer service. Especially when you're the one who's wrong, and the client is totally, irrevocably, and absolutely right.

The customer's complaints *"You and your company were late, you left us hanging"* and, *"You didn't even call a warning or alert, or admit that you screwed up when we still had time to modify the ad and go to another supplier for a replacement item. What your company did, was ignore us. You and your people knew we'd be damaged if you failed to deliver on time, but that didn't matter! There doesn't seem to be any reason for us to continue to do business with you as a supplier. You guys are lousy at customer service. You're poor communicators, and you darn sure didn't even care enough to notify us that there was a problem until it was too late for us to do anything about it."*

Ouch. You can hardly blame them for being upset. So you got an ear-full and were soundly and roundly described as a poor quality supplier that doesn't know how to manage timing for what should have been a simple on-time delivery. That sums up the disaster. Most of what they said was wrong, but you don't want to start a fight. They were venting. They have every right.

Then you presented your proposed solution, which might, just might pull this off. But the fact that they still don't know, is certainly not helping the atmosphere. And if you do manage to survive this disaster you're going to have to bend over backwards to rebuild their confidence in both you, *and* your company.

The question remaining is, what can you say, and what can be done to assuage the situation? How do you say or do anything that soothes a rightfully upset customer? You know that simply saying you're sorry, doesn't help.

Naturally you respond to the customer *immediately*. This means right now, not tomorrow or next week. *Immediately*. Face to face if at all possible!

No excuse is adequate. Weekend coming up? Busy with something else? Too bad! What ever delays you, destroys you right now, and destroys your company and its reputation for the future.

Even a short delay severely and adversely affects your status as the ultimately responsible individual.

You did that. Actually you've tried to do all of the right stuff.

At this point, all that you can do is formally extend your apologies for the error and state that your response is not a token or "quickie" effort, but is a sincere demonstration of the customer's importance to you and your company. And you let them know that revised scheduling details are being implemented as paramount.

Apologies are important. Be specific in your acknowledgement so that the client knows you *really* understand the severity of the problem. Deliver a *genuine apology*. Forget trying to lay the blame on somebody else. That just makes you look weak and untrustworthy

"Playing the blame game never works. A deep set of research shows that people who blame others for their mistakes lose status, learn less, and perform worse relative to those who own up to their mistakes. Research also shows that the same applies for organizations. Groups and organizations with a rampant culture of blame have a serious disadvantage when it comes to creativity, learning, innovation, and productive risk-taking." Nathanael J. Fast, Harvard Business Review®

Yes, you screwed up. But you learned from it. You're knocking yourself out to fix the problem. You're not the only person who's ever screwed up. Top management has screwed up. The client has screwed up. The fact that they're where they are today is a testament to the fact that they learned from their mistakes and didn't get pissy.

Take a deep breath. Stay calm. Stay logical. You can do this.

He who lives in harmony
with himself, lives in harmony
with the universe.

Marcus Aurelius

Chapter 11

Work/Life Balance
or
Work/Life Harmony

Chapter 11

Work / Life Balance – Work/Life Harmony

Jeff Bezos, Chairman, President, and CEO of Amazon, (the global company had 566,000 employees in 2017), takes issue with the term work-life balance. Instead he proposes that work-life _harmony_ makes more sense. The term work-life _balance_ implies an equal division of time between two competing elements, which, in most cases never actually happens.

Bezos posits that work and life actually comprise a circle. Grasping the concept that harmony as opposed to balance can be important to the future of your business, so too does harmony affect your ability for growth and development as a business leader. At the same time you are required to fulfill a leading professional role, the same needs and constraints can be expected to affect your job as husband and father, wife and mother, caregiver, or any other role in your personal life.

Additionally, getting 8 hours of sleep every night remains critical to both you and Bezos, who says that "_If you shortchange your sleep, you might get in a couple of productive hours, but that productivity might be an illusion._" He also noted that "_When you're talking about decisions and_ *interactions, quality is usually more important than quantity."*

He's right. Time is adjustable to the nature of event, decision and thought. The one thing you can say for certain is that time cannot be parceled out in fixed quantities. Certainly not when a crisis arises, or when someone needs your input.

The "circle" Bezos speaks of permits (*up to 24 hours in a day*) your moving in and out of every decision-making meeting and each thought processing session, while continually recognizing the requirements and obligations required by and of, your family. There also needs to be thought given to allotting your personal time and clearly thinking about just what it is that you personally need (beyond the requisite 8 hours of nightly sleep) for your mental and emotional well-being.

The goal is to keep it all together, including designating adequate numbers of seconds, minutes and hours to and for every component system part. This has to happen every day, week, month and year as well. Yes, it is intimidating, and, it is complex. But, no one promised a "silver bullet" cure for all the world's ills, and no one said it would be easy to accomplish.

In his own search for work-life harmony, Jeff Bezos and his wife, married since 1993 and with four active children, all enjoy having breakfast together. Bezos makes it a point to never schedule early morning meetings at Amazon in order to preserve that family time.

Additionally, until 2013, Mackenzie Bezos drove their children to school in the family's Honda, then dropped her husband off at the office, after which she went to her own job, as an accountant for Amazon. Today she is an award-winning author who works from her home office until it's time to pick the children up from school. In 2014, Mackenzie Bezos founded the anti-bullying organization *Bystander Revolution*, where she serves as executive director.

According to an interview with Vogue, the family shares off-season travel, they engage in kitchen-science experiments, chicken incubation, Mandarin lessons, and the Singapore math program. The Bezos children are also active in clubs and sports with other neighborhood kids.

Starting with work, you need to be energized and excited to accomplish needed results each and every day, and you need to be ready to face the toughest problems. At the same time, you also have to meet the very real needs of those people who work for you, as well as the people around you. You must react to the people who oversee your own work and still, you have to deal with all the demands of family, children, husband, wife, significant other, or parents.

The teaching or joint collaboration with your people at home and at work is a demand that you either face or hide from, depending upon the energy reserve you have at the requirement's arrival time, when action is needed.

Can you respond to your children's need for guidance in addition to simply dispensing the occasional hug? How about your spouse or significant other? How about the administrative assistants, phone answering folks and, what about top management?

Do you get tired just thinking about trying to face each and every one, garbed in what you hope to be the appropriate persona, when at the same time you haven't the slightest idea if what you're proposing is correct, or for that matter if what you're proposing is appropriately packaged for likely implementation by the recipient? Frankly, you're not alone.

Your teachers, at every level you attended, from basic elementary school through sophisticated graduate schools, were faced with the same dilemma. They likely thought to themselves, *What should I tell watching, listening, breathlessly waiting (or totally oblivious) students which will convey meaningful, thought-provoking, and challenging input?* The sub-text of that thought, of course, is the frustrating realization that *based on the looks on some of their uncomprehending little faces, you'd think that I was conducting this class in Chinese.*

If you are clearer thinking than they are, you might stand a chance of passing along a small portion of the gems of knowledge you're attempting to impart. It's a long way of saying, *They can make notes and they can rely on memory, but the important thing is for me to get one or possibly two messages across in a single 50 minute period.*

Once upon a time students hungered for knowledge that would help either erase or enliven lives which were lived without any of the modern conveniences we currently take for granted. The reality is that today's children are growing and developing into regular people and during the "formative" period, it is difficult to get their attention, much less hold it for a protracted (or even momentary) period of time.

Granted Jeff Bezos is both a hard act to follow, and one that doesn't have a lot of parallels with any of us – either economically or in terms of his life style, but he does seem to have identified not just the right idea, but the right phrase; work-life harmony.

So let's think about this... Many people are so busy working that they've actually forgotten how to enjoy life. They never take time for themselves. As a result, they're too busy to find time to play, and the job that used to be not just intellectually stimulating but downright fun, has become just another mundane responsibility.

A while back, Harvard Business School reported the results of a survey in which 94% of working professionals said they were working more than 50 hours per week, and nearly half of those surveyed reported putting in more than 65 hours a week. - Forbes

Your ability to produce tends to level off because you're not feeling the challenge, the sport, the triumph, the pride you always used to feel when you nailed another great deal. And by the time you get home, you're so tired all you really want to do is eat dinner, maybe watch a little TV, surf the web for a few minutes, and fall sleep. Heavenly sleep. Escape. The thing is, you never actually feel fully rested anymore. And forget about your relationship. Who even has time?

And then there's a stack of bills on the counter you just don't want to have to face today. The money's there, or maybe its not. It's just the effort to deal with the ones that are not automatically deducted that seems beyond you at the moment. Maybe a nap will help.

Face it. Your work-life harmony is WAY out of sync. Of course, you're not the only one. So what do the professionals suggest?

That actually depends. If the bottom line is that you really do like your job but you're a borderline burnout candidate, it's time to cut back on some of those hours and carve out a little "me-time." Think of it as a sanity break. It's time to reward yourself. You work hard, you deserve to enjoy some of the fruits of your labor. Decide what you'd enjoy. A massage? Roller-blading? Jogging? A work-out at the gym? A trip to the beach? A half-day fishing trip? A visit to the nursery for a trunk full of flowers to brighten up the yard or the patio? What about a trip to the local animal shelter? It's good for your head. You might even decide to come home with a new best friend.

On the other hand, if you're not totally wild about your job but the money's good, once again, you can reward yourself with a hobby. Ease back on the hours and do something you seriously enjoy.

Working late an hour or two every night? Cut that number in half. Seriously. Just do it. Arrive a little early instead if you think you really need to put that total amount of time in. The idea is to get you out of there at decent time in the afternoon so that that time now belongs to you and only you.

Take up a hobby. There are tons of them. Paint, write, sculpt, body-build, martial-arts, dancing, surfing, collecting, or maybe learn a foreign language, take an interesting course, you name it.

137

Reduce stress. Do something to benefit your body. Need to lose some weight? That might make you feel better. Set very, very modest goals. Choose a single item and eliminate it from your diet until your body no longer craves it, then choose another and eliminate that one. Yes, you can exercise if you like, but this is simple and you won't be straining your body with exercise until it's much lighter. It's really quite simple. The point is to whittle down the amount of carbohydrates you're consuming. Lists of food containing carbohydrates are online. If you're cheerfully snarking a giant bowl of ice cream every night, just stop. Eat an apple. If you're eating a mountain of white bread, stop that instead. There are a ton of good tasting low-carb bread options. You can also bake them yourself. That's it. Nothing dramatic.

Are you overworked? Try delegating some of those tasks. Wasting time online? No need to stop, just budget your time so it's not 2AM when it finally occurs to you that 6:30AM is going to roll around way too soon. Allow yourself a half hour. Or an hour. You know your own schedule. You're smart, you can do this. Use the time you're not spending on that for something positive.

Read a bedtime-story to a kid. Don't have one underfoot? Pick up the phone. Or read it a spouse. Or to the cat. Cats LOVE to hear bedtime-stories. So do dogs.

138

Work-Life Balance or Work-Life Harmony. Call it whatever you want.

You've got this.

Sources for Jeff Bezos info. – Vogue Magazine, Business Insider, Wikipedia

Stay ahead of the curve.
Monitor upcoming trends
in your field of business.

Chapter 12

Proactively Reactive

Chapter 12

Proactively Reactive

This may well seem like an oxymoron, but if you stop and think about it (obviously I did) it makes total sense. Being able to anticipate occurrences before they happen, can be a wonderful attribute. I'm not talking about knowing the winning Powerball® numbers before they're picked (although that would be nice), I mean having advance knowledge of upcoming trends in your business along with the business-savvy that allows you to maximize your opportunities.

I found this to be critical as a manufacturing rep. I was able to secure product lines to sell before they became household names. Granted, I wasn't always right, but you don't have to be. A ten percent success rate is better than 100% afterthought.

You do not need to own a crystal ball to have a glimpse into the future, you just need to know which of the individual businesses in a field of particular interest is likely to come up with exciting new products. You need to be able to look into their bag of tricks, forecast what specific device might be coming, estimate how soon, and envision the ability for it to become the next ultra-attractive purchase for hundreds of thousands of consumers.

Sounds simple. It's not. Granted it's simpler today than it used to be. Originally, for a marketing rep to become even peripherally aware of a development waiting in the wings, I'd have told you that you must have a passion for a specific segment of a particular industry. You would have to understand and then befriend an individual who was actively working in that industry in order to be aware of developments that were once only a dream until they were designed, built, tested and assembled, turned into tomorrow's newest and most consumer-attractive gadgets or gizmos.

Adding expanded capabilities to existing products can bring the glitter of gold to something the public might have earlier taken for granted. For example, the cell phone, initially seen as granting freedom from having to wait by a land-line for an important call, was greeted with a sigh of relief and nothing further was expected. Then came smartphones and other hand held devices, which were met with wild enthusiasm, and overnight they became part of their lives. This happened without most of the world having even a rudimentary grasp of the technology that makes it all work.

The advantage of knowing who might be developing a product which has substantial benefit potential for you and your employer or board of directors, would require that you establish a relationship with individual developers.

Naturally, in nearly every instance there must a significant element of trust. You must convince the inventor that you will retain only what is needed to market the idea brought to fruition. The developer has to believe that you can be close-mouthed and devoid of the intent to take the benefits of his or her work and use it as a personal tool.

The entire process requires patience, skill and awareness of the details of what it might be that consumers see as important and necessary. Anticipation is difficult but it can be hugely rewarding. It tests skills, courage and silence that separate you from non-aware competition. It's not unlike a reporter having a trusted source for an important story that will eventually become front page news.

This style of one-on-one relationship with an employee of a manufacturing entity is still sound, but non-disclosure agreements usually prevent any information from leaking out until the company itself decides to make an announcement.

Another way to stay ahead of the curve is to subscribe to the services of one of the companies like Crimson Hexagon®, which specializes in industry-specific intelligence. Not only will that information provide the industry-specific information you were searching for, it may also introduce you to new technology that has the ability to streamline operations of your own, or your client's business. Passing that information along to a client has the additional benefit of letting them know that you have the well-being of their business at heart.

For example, *"An extension of the foundational algorithm of the Crimson Hexagon Platform, BrightView for Customer Care accurately identifies and processes customer communications from any source — social media, emails, chat logs, call transcripts — so they can be routed to the proper system, dramatically reducing time to issue discovery and resolution."* That's a pretty good idea. Worth passing along for evaluation by a client.

For industry or product specific matters; *"Crimson Hexagon's AI-powered consumer insights platform analyzes online consumer conversations from social media, reviews, forums, and provides the insights consumer electronics brands need to launch innovative products and successful campaigns that resonate with their target audience."*

In one study – *"By analyzing consumer conversations with Crimson Hexagon, FOCUS® brands learned that, although Starbucks® and Panera® were frequently mentioned in the overall iced green tea conversation, no brands were talking about mango-flavored iced green tea. After testing messaging, FOCUS Brands launched the new mango iced green tea to a highly positive reception. It has been a popular menu item ever since."*

In short this is targeted knowledge. Data which provides clients, regardless of whether they are service related, manufacturers, or sales specialists, with timely and specific customer-centric information on what customers like and hate about a product, and what shortcomings or approvals need to be quickly addressed by a manufacturer (or competitor) in order to maintain or gain product share. The salient points from that information can also be incorporated into marketing campaigns, playing to the product's strong points, the ones most sought by consumers.

From a manufacturer's standpoint, in order to determine how to proceed with the information you have been furnished, and then assess the potential of a proposed product, you will need to develop a cadre of technical people, marketing folks and funded visionaries who can evaluate, often without seeing a finished product, postulate what will be there, and project approximately when it will arrive. It may well come kicking and screaming into the world like any newborn, but, having done your research, once off to the right start, that proposed product can grow to become a full blown delight to consumers.

Simple ideas can generate millions. If you learn to recognize them.

Todd Green started losing his hair in his 20's, so he decided the heck with it, and tried shaving his remaining hair off with a traditional razor. It did not go well.

"If I could just take a blade and put it in my hand," he thought, "it would be a much easier, more intuitive way to shave." Green came up with a prototype in 1998, hired a designer to help him perfect it, borrowed money from family and friends, found a manufacturer, then built his own website and taught himself e-commerce and marketing. Time magazine named HeadBlade® one of the best designs in 2000, and his product really took off.

Actor Yul Brynner (Westworld, The King and I) was average looking. Then he shaved his head. And he became a sex symbol.

Actor Sir Patrick Stewart (Captain Jean Luc Picard /Star Trek®) began losing his hair at the age of 19. With a toupee he was average looking. Bald, he's a sex symbol.

Actor Aristotle "Telly" Savalas shaved his head in 1965. He began playing Detective Kojack in 1973. "Once I became bald," a puzzled Savalas said, "women seemed to find me more attractive."

A 2015 article in Huffington Post® was entitled "Thank You, Bruce Willis, For Making Bald Beautiful." Bruce Willis had a great head of hair in his early "Moonlighting" days, but by the mid-80's his hairline had already begun to recede. It made him look old. He later wore his hair in buzz cut in a few movies, but in 2010 for the movie "Red" he shaved it. And it looked good. Really good. Really, REALLY good. It also enhanced his status as a sex symbol.

My own hair was just about gone after college, so the idea of being thought of as a sex symbol was met with great enthusiasm.

It was discovered that women had viewed bald men as having "a kind of badass loveable rogue-ness about them." And men finally took notice. Suddenly they felt as if they actually had a choice. And this kind of choice was particularly appealing.

Dwayne Johnson (The Rock) looked OK with hair. But he looked even better without it. He made the choice to shave his head somewhere around 2010. When asked why, he quipped, "I'm not bald because I went bald. I'm bald because my hair is a cross between an afro and hair from a llama's ball sac."

In 2017 researchers at the University of Pennsylvania released the results of a survey which determined that women found bald men more attractive. Bald men were perceived as more dominant, and the study also indicated that bald men will do better in business and economically overall. The researchers suggested that instead of spending billions each year trying to reverse or cure their hair loss, men experiencing male pattern baldness should consider shaving their heads. It would likely be a rewarding experience.

Todd Green's HeadBlade was an intuitive invention, originally designed for his own use, but he immediately recognized its financial potential. Today his product is everywhere. And he's a very wealthy man.

Learn to look at the world with an eye toward marketing potential.

Be Proactively Reactive.

The old school of thought
was not to mix
business and pleasure.

Chapter 13

Don't Mix Business And Pleasure

Chapter 13

Don't Mix Business and Pleasure

OK, let's get the obvious out of the way first. You go to work, you meet people. You might find yourself attracted to someone in the office. Whether you realize it or not, this happens to be VERY obvious to everybody else in the office, regardless of how discrete you think you're being.

This is also very obvious to everyone in the office even if one person is based in another city and only flies in to your branch periodically on business.

If the other person is married, you have just subjected the entire office to an Excedrin® headache. This will not end well. For anybody.

If both of you are single and you hit it off, somebody is probably going to suggest that the two of you get a room, because even if you're twenty feet away from each other the sparks are still perfectly visible to everybody else.

If the relationship is not working, somebody has to pull the plug. One of three things is likely to happen. Either one party is going to be in agony, silently suffering from heartache, unable to heal because the proximity between you remains the same, or one party is going to try to get the other fired so as not to be further inconvenienced, or, one party is going to discover he's been dating Glenn Close from "Fatal Attraction."

In actuality, 30% of office romances do end up in marriage. The other 70% of those who have engaged in office romances are given the opportunity to reflect on a valuable lesson as they search for a new job.

Another problem with office relationships is the potential for jealousy to rear its ugly head in the workplace. Friendly banter between people of the opposite sex can be mistaken for flirting, leaving the impression that someone is attempting to encroach upon your territory. And unless you have a metal detector and a guard at the front door… well, let's just say that nobody needs that kind of drama in the office.

OK yes, some of the 30% of office relationships that do end up in marriage turn out to be very happy, but for the most part, even if the company is OK with it, one of the pair needs to find another job, because face it…you'll end up talking business all the time, and have nothing to share with each other at the end of the day. This is not good for sustaining a relationship.

Marriage between two employees in the same business often makes for an awkward relationship with co-workers. It automatically generates a feeling of unease, because whatever you say to one person in confidence is still going to be shared with the other, which is not exactly what you had intended.

A boss/employee romantic relationship is one which is particularly fraught with danger. Sexual harassment suits are definitely on the rise.

I can think of only one office romance that turned out exceptionally well. A young VP, a Princeton graduate, worked at D.E. Shaw, an investment firm. He was one of several people at the firm who interviewed a potential new hire, a 23 year old girl who was a fellow Princeton grad. She was eventually hired by the firm and H.R. assigned her to the office next to his. She later confessed that she found herself enchanted by his laugh, and decided to make the first move by asking him out to lunch. They were engaged in three months, married in six. When he told her he wanted to quit, move to another state, and start his own company, she quit her job as well. His start-up hired her as the fledgling company's accountant. The young couple eventually had four children. She juggled work with motherhood until her third son was born, and then gave her full concentration to the kids as a stay-at-home mom. She tried to squeeze in some "me-time" over the ten year period it took her to write her first book. It took eight years to write her second one. Kids are pretty demanding. But the marriage worked out, the children were healthy and happy, the business was successful, and her books were well received.   Very few office romances turn out to have such happy endings. Or together earn such huge amounts of money.

The old school of thought was "Don't mix business and pleasure." That really is still true relative to extracurricular activities in the work place (*Let me reiterate that message one more time; No screwing around with your subordinates.*)

On the other hand...

There is no better way to develop and build relationships with clients than to get out of the office and do something that both of you enjoy. Fun.

As a subscriber to that school of thought, I believe people like to do business with folks whose company they enjoy, and creating friendships and relationships with business associates happens to be best facilitated out of the office environment. As it happens, some of my longest lasting business relationships have been built by socializing with clients outside of work. Some of these developed further, becoming hard and fast friendships which are still going strong over a period of more than 20 years.

Defining realities clarifies mysteries. Mixing business with pleasure combines your work and social life. You get friendly with those you do business with.

These relationships have advantages too – for example, when you need an important issue resolved, you can communicate your needs and requirements in a comfortable fashion with someone you and they both consider as a friend.

A casual conversation with a business associate can start a friendship. A discussion of non-business related subjects, even such things as briefly mentioning something about your personal or private life can be one way to further a growing relationship, but choosing to do so can also be fraught with danger.

There are friends and there are friends. Get to know each other well enough before you even think about spilling your innermost secrets, because business relationships, no matter how much you like another individual, still require professionalism and mutual respect. There's also the matter of finding something you may have confided to a business friend, being casually shared with that person's spouse or significant other. In short, your personal business could be casually related to someone who feels no loyalty to you, when it comes to sharing what might be considered a juicy piece of gossip. It's wise to be prudent. Some things are best kept to yourself.

Caution is also needed so that there is very little if any judging by either. Your concentration should be on finding common non-business related ground. Football. Baseball. Tennis. Soccer. Golf.

Fishing. Boating. Collecting. Woodworking. Art. History. Museums. Movies. Travel. Classic Cars. Bikes. Pets. Remodeling. Even what you'd do if you won the lottery. There are a lot of conversational options, and these are only a few.

Too much friendliness, even with professional colleagues can lead to judging and eventual distrust. When you learn about another's foibles, at the same time, you have an increased risk of your knowledge of those same foibles ruining a friendship, and as well, a colleague to colleague business relationship.

Thus, there is good news and there is bad news. Mixing business with pleasure is an important part of your position. But, remember that mixing business with pleasure also is fraught with pitfalls that are hard to avoid falling into, and are difficult if not impossible to recover from. Seek friendships external to your workplace and control yourself with colleagues that you do business with on a regular basis. The aim here is to develop long-term friendships, not one night stands.

Here's another facet of the business / pleasure discussion. If you travel on business, there's either somebody waiting for you to return, or someone thinking about you in your absence. If you finish up your appointment early and your plane doesn't leave until later, or perhaps even the following day, why not take a look at what the points of interest are in that area, then share that part of your trip with someone else. A sibling, one of your own kids, a husband, a wife, a significant other, or friends on Facebook®.

You can snap and post pictures as you wander through interesting places, adding thoughts and observations as you go. You're not alone, you're accompanied by people who find what you're seeing and doing fascinating, and they'll tell you so in real time. Chances are it may be the only time some of those people have ever seen what you're showing them. Technology, the smartphone in your pocket or your bag, has provided you with the opportunity to both give and derive pleasure while you're on a solo business trip.

The top travel destinations for business in the U.S. are Chicago, San Francisco, and New York, but there's also an uptick in business travel to Philadelphia, Phoenix, Salt Lake, Louisville, Las Vegas, Denver, West Palm Beach, Atlanta, and Miami, to name only a few. Regardless of where you're headed, there are lots of interesting places to go, and things to see and do, many of which are free.

And don't forget the food. As a road warrior, I made it a point to "eat local." Buffalo chicken wings, Philly cheesesteak, Chicago deep dish pizza, KC BBQ, Maine lobster, etc, etc.

There are also some very strange things that visitors to those cities often find interesting. Official city websites often point out particularly intriguing points of interest. So does Trip Advisor. More creative, however, is the AtlasObscura website.

Take their Chicago entry, for example, *"Some people post handmade signs to remind dog owners to be mindful of where their pets do their business, but one Chicago artist decided to make his statement with a permanent bronze sculpture known quite simply as the, "Shit Fountain."* No, actually, I'm not kidding, and surely that's something the folks back home haven't yet seen.

There are a ton of other free and cheap things to see and do in Chicago. According to the Driehaus Foundation website, you can chat with talking statues.

"Statue Stories Chicago is a free, city-wide arts initiative in which Chicago's most celebrated writers, actors, and comedians were commissioned to write and voice monologues for 30 statues across the city. The statues "speak" when a smartphone scans a QR code (or it is typed into a browser) on a sign next to the statue. When the phone rings, visitors receive a "call back" from John C. Reilly as Abraham Lincoln or Steve Carell as Man With Fish at the Shedd Aquarium, to name just a few. Together they tell Chicago's story."

So about that well known caveat about not mixing business with pleasure... well, clearly one has to determine what constitutes pleasure.

And then you can share it.

When winners lose
they do it like Winners.

Chapter 14

Learn How To Lose

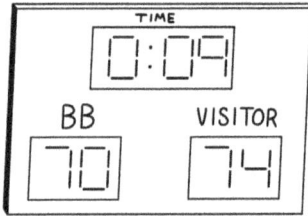

Chapter 14

Learn How To Lose

Kareem Abdul Jabbar is an extremely articulate ex NBA superstar. His commentaries transcend the fact that he held basketball scoring records for many years, and during his time at UCLA he made college basketball history.

Kareem had many wonderful quotes, but the one that remained with me is:

"*You cannot win unless you learn how to lose*"

Its meaning encompasses the fact that you can't appreciate winning until you have lost. Losing drives you to succeed. It pushes you to be better. So, according to the well-known 19th-century proverb, *If at first you don't succeed, try, try again.* That's a truism for sales, as well as for life.

When you do lose – and you certainly will – learn to lose with grace and humility. Lose gracefully like a winner. This is important stuff, because a winner has confidence, and that confidence is part of him or her. It is inculcated within the personality of a winner to be able to take a loss with the spirit of a champion.

Very rare indeed is the loser in a major match who walks off without hugging and/or patting the back of the winning player, congratulating the opponent and acknowledging the win. Losing like a champion teaches you how to win like a champion! Sales and life are a close fit when it comes to winning or losing. Losing gracefully is not just humbling, but it's an honorable loss, which maintains the real truth right alongside the burning desire to win. Losing like a loser is something that can be outgrown, but in the meantime, it makes you look like a total fool.

I am impressed by how much can be learned by living and experiencing the multitude of small, artful acts which add up. Winning isn't everything – it is certainly important, both in life and in business. But for every win there is a loss. This is also important stuff to be conscious of as well.

Including the need to express oneself honestly, goes with living honestly. Note that living honestly makes it easier to grasp winning, and honesty is a giant step toward achieving a goal.

Honesty isn't a sometime thing. Having honesty to guide your words allows you to speak the truth – not reserving the hard-to-say things. The hard points are the ones that are difficult for all of us to speak, and harder to issue even when they are fully deserved.

Life, and people's feelings are real, and somewhat fragile. We all strive for a balance between speech and silence. The silence is often reserved so as to keep from honestly speaking, when by doing so, one might inadvertently wound a fragile ego, harm a relationship, or damage an important camaraderie. Sometimes, keeping quiet is simply the right thing to do.

The role of this book is to help. This chapter is intended to teach that disappointment can be accepted, without weakening your focus on the positive side of winning. There is a temptation to bring self-pity to the forefront but a caveat dictates the necessity of keeping self-pity away from things that guide or rule our lives. The nature of self-pity is that you can lose yourself in it. The risk is using it to indulge our non-productive, minimally alive emotional side.

The end result is that once again, while winning isn't everything, for some, it's all that counts, which is why we need to learn how to lose with grace and humility. Being a good sport actually allows us to ascend a notch in the opinion of others.

Occasionally we have the dubious honor of watching people make absolute asses of themselves in front of the entire world, instead of losing (or winning) gracefully.

Regardless of the specific venue, sports, the workplace, personal, political or what-have-you, the underlying reaction to any given situation provides us with a bird's-eye-view of a person's character. We are all judged on the quality of our character, or lack thereof.

In 2004, as he was being handed an award, singer Elton John took the microphone, and in his acceptance speech he insulted another contestant to whom he had just lost a more prestigious award. "Madonna, best live act?" he said. "F--- off. Since when has lip-syncing been 'live'? Sorry about that, but I think everyone who lip-syncs on stage in public, when you pay like 75 quid to see them, should be shot. Thank you very much. That's me off her Christmas card list, but do I give a toss? No."

Elton John left his audience with their collective jaws agape, and their minds likely thinking "What. A. Jerk!"

During the Athens Olympics in 2004 the talented two-time champion, Svetlana Khorkina lost the women's all-around competition to a 16 year old U.S. gymnast named Carly Patterson. Instead of losing gracefully, Khorkina publicly blamed the judges, and complained that she likely lost because of her nationality. "I think it's because I'm from Russia, not from America," she told a reporter from the U.S. "I've seen much tougher competition than her," she continued. "Let's see how long she can remain on top. Can she keep going and compete in two more Olympics like myself?" Sounded more like sour grapes.

When the infamous Anthony Weiner experienced an embarrassing loss in a New York Mayoral

Primary, he exited his election night party and greeted waiting photographers by shooting a bird at them. His petulant gesture was caught on video. He could just as easily have smiled, waved, shrugged, said "Win some, lose some" and left the waiting press with a positive impression. But, no.

In 2012, Gary Smith, a New Mexico congressional candidate, was arrested after allegedly slashing all four tires of the woman who was his primary opponent. It's not as if the race had even been close. He took 3% of the vote. He was simply a sore loser. Filled with resentment, he decided to take his frustration out on the winner. A security camera caught him in the act. If he applied to you for a job, would you hire him? Surely not after that display.

California Congressional Representative Duncan Hunter was arrested and charged with dozens of counts of campaign finance fraud. The list of personal purchases using campaign funds was startling to say the least. He spent the money on lavish foreign vacations, personal flights for friends and family, golf forays, clothing, a $600 plane ticket for a pet rabbit, a big supply of golf balls, expensive meals, thirty shots of tequila, over thirty thousand dollars in bank overdraft fees, and so on. When caught, he insisted that everyone else was to blame. He blamed the opposing political party, he blamed his wife, he blamed his children, he blamed the pet bunny rabbit... OK, you get the picture.

Does this fall into the category of "losing?" In a manner of speaking, yes. The Congressman felt entitled, and he expected to continue to be able to get away with keeping his hand in the cookie jar. He was losing. And he deserved to lose.

Happily, there are those who do handle losing gracefully.

37 year old Los Angeles Dodgers pitcher Rich Hill just missed throwing a no-hitter against the Pittsburgh Pirates in 2017. He also just lost out on a perfect game when his third baseman made an error in the ninth inning. He didn't rant about the teammate who caused him to lose out on a perfect game. Instead, when he spoke to the press, an upbeat Hill said, "I'm looking forward to tomorrow, getting in the gym and getting ready for the next outing. We have a lot of great things going on here," Hill said. "Tomorrow is a big game. We have to take the series and get back home."

There was a hotly contested political Primary election, where each of the candidates for Governor was considered well qualified. All had held political office previously. Three of the four were multi-millionaires. It was the fourth candidate who prevailed, however. Of the three multi-millionaires, all of whom had spent tens of millions of their own money during the campaign, this is the way each of them handled their losing;

The first multi-millionaire spoke from the podium - "[My opponent] and I have been friends for a very long time," she said. "We were friends before this race began, we are friends today, and we will be friends in the future…Now, go out and win this damned thing."

The second had his campaign release a statement which read, "I wish [my opponent]… luck as our party works together to defeat [our opponents] at the polls in November. Let's make history, and make [my opponent] the next Governor of [my state]."

The third sent a personal email to every registered voter in his political party as well as the Independents who supported him. Here's what his letter said;

"I want to thank all of our supporters, volunteers, and staff who made this journey possible. You sacrificed so much and I'll always be humbled and thankful for your love and your labor.

Each of my primary opponents had the guts to step into the arena, to run and push forward the values and ideas that will move our state forward. That's what our democracy is all about.

Today, we end our campaign the same way we started, with our heads high and our hearts full—and with a renewed determination to fight for the state we love.

I want to congratulate [my opponent] on his victory, emerging as the leader of our party as our state's nominee for Governor.

My opponent is a fierce fighter who has what it takes to lead our state forward, and he can count on my help every step of the way. I may not be your next Governor, but that won't stop me from fighting for our state with a new attitude and a bright future.

This is a fight for the future of our state and the soul of our nation, and it's a fight that we are going to win. We must stand together and make our voices heard."

This message from that third candidate, who had spent 20% of his personal net wealth (which was a LOT) on the campaign, exhibited what is called losing with grace and dignity.

He also managed to leave recipients of his letter with the impression that he is an honest-to-goodness class act. Should he run for Congress or the Senate in the next election, voters will already have a very positive opinion of him. They've just seen him in action. Add that to his prior political record, a good one, and whatever he chooses to do next, he will already have established himself as worthy of voter's respect.

Occasionally losing is a fact of life. It's the way that you do it that counts.

Get involved...
and benefit.

Chapter 15

Networking

Chapter 15

Networking

This category is so obvious as to almost be unworthy of discussion. But, I'm always amazed at how many people fail to take advantage of the numerous networking opportunities available to them. In my career, I made it a point to be heavily involved in my trade association (Consumer Technology Association.)

The more I got involved, the more I benefited from my membership. Business opportunities, connection resources, personal growth, there is a long list of benefits. Networking is simply great for this. When you network, you give and, you receive. Get involved and benefit. Take advantage of this opportunity. It helps you and, it helps your company. Not a "joiner"? This may be the one step you can take into an entire new world.

There are trade associations related to a myriad of industries, and if you're not yet involved in your own, you definitely want to take a look. Think, for example of how many branches and related industries of your own field there are.

Consider just about any business and you can rattle off components or divisions which will either directly interact, service, compliment, or mesh with your own industry or interests. You may also discover that trade associations other than your own specific niche, offer additional opportunities to network

At these events you have the ability to meet and interact with people who may be involved with materials sourcing, component manufacturing, recycling, new and used machinery, industry specific tools, transportation, storage, software, printing, advertising, copywriting, editing, product retailers, wholesalers, travel, shipping, vehicle sales and rentals, computing devices, smartphones, real estate, webmasters, event planners, speakers bureaus, publishing, trade shows, furnishings, fixtures, etc. etc. etc.

How about hobbies? There are hobby groups where people who share your recreational interests gather. Does your business offer a product or service that might be of interest or assistance to others in that group? You can easily combine business with pleasure here. The point of the exercise is to get acquainted with people, enjoy yourself, and maybe have the opportunity to pick up a little business at the same time.

Even better are social clubs or groups which provide a public service. Many social organizations have specific services or charities they are known for supporting. These organizations provide superb networking opportunities with members who have at their core a genuine desire to make this world a better place.

For example;

"**Shriners International** Headquarters® is a fraternity based on fun, fellowship and the Masonic principles of brotherly love, relief and truth. The fraternity is open to men of integrity from all walks of life."

"Shriners Hospitals for Children is committed to providing specialized care to children with orthopaedic conditions, burns, spinal cord injuries, cleft lip and palate, and certain other special health care needs, regardless of the families' ability to pay." The Shriners also offer clean and well maintained retirement facilities for their elderly members.

"**Lions Club International®** is the world's largest service club organization. It provides diabetes education and offers a summer camp for children with diabetes. They're bullish on the environment, with a focus on clean water and planting trees. They help families of children with cancer, distribute food to schoolchildren, stock food banks, create sustainable community gardens, and lead community food drives to fight hunger where they live and work. They screen vision, educate communities, build clinics and support the blind and visually impaired through assistive technology and vocational training programs."

"**Rotary Club International®** - Through Rotary clubs, 1.2 million people from all continents and cultures come together to exchange ideas, and form friendships and professional connections. Rotary Club causes are listed on the club's information page as; Promote Peace, Fight Disease, Provide Clean Water, Support Education, Save Mothers and Children, and Grow Local Economies. Rotary is a leading partner in the Global Polio Eradication Initiative. With help from partners, the Bill & Melinda Gates Foundation, the World Health Organization, the U.S. Centers for Disease Control and Prevention, and UNICEF. Rotary has helped make the world 99.9 percent polio-free. Rotary is involved with Disaster Relief; Rotary and ShelterBox collaborate to provide emergency shelter and vital supplies to stabilize, protect, and support communities affected by disasters and humanitarian crises."

"Unity for Service **The National Exchange Club®** is the only service organization exclusively serving communities in the United States. More than 650 local clubs throughout the U.S. and Puerto Rico provide individuals with opportunities to use their time and talents to benefit their local communities and the country as a whole. Exchange Clubs Core Values are family, community, and country. The Exchange Club's national project is the prevention of child abuse."

"**Kiwanis Club International®** is a global organization of volunteers dedicated to improving the world, one child and one community at a time.

Each year, Kiwanis clubs sponsor nearly 150,000 service projects, complete more than 18.5 million hours in volunteer service and raise more than $100 million. As a global project in coordination with UNICEF, members and clubs contributed more than $80 million toward the global elimination of iodine deficiency disorders (IDD), the leading preventable cause of mental retardation. Beginning in 2010 Kiwanis International joined with UNICEF to launch a new worldwide health initiative, The Eliminate Project, dedicated to wiping out maternal and neonatal tetanus (MNT), which kills more than 100,000 babies worldwide each year."

"**Optimist International®** is made up of autonomous Optimist Clubs that do work in their communities. Each club independently raises funds, and chooses service projects to improve the lives of children. Examples of typical projects include sponsoring youth athletic leagues, holding essay and oratorical contests for scholarships, and supporting local schools."

Other opportunities for networking include multi-day conferences which are excellent places to network. There is ample time to get to know people, to grab a cup of coffee, have lunch, or dinner together, or in a group. The ice has already been broken because you're all learning something together. Additionally, conference speakers themselves are often very good candidates to network with.

And don't forget "Meet-Ups" Every metro area has them, and they span a wide variety of interests. You can even start one yourself!

I'm a big proponent of trade shows...and they come in all shapes on sizes. Two I'm most familiar with are CES and ECRM.

"The International Consumer Electronics Show (CES) is an annual trade show organized by the Consumer Technology Association. Held in January at the Las Vegas Convention Center in Las Vegas, Nevada, United States, the event typically hosts presentations of new products and technologies in the consumer electronics industry."

CES is the world's largest trade event encompassing all facets of the technology world. The traditional booth size is 10'x 10' and they go up from there, to displays which are the size of a small city (well, almost.) This environment, while not a traditional networking event, does offer many opportunities during the show to do just that. I've found that to be the case with most trade events. Open cocktail parties flourish and you can pick your spots based not only on who the sponsor is but on the audience you want to network with. Of course the traffic (hopefully) at your booth also allows for the meeting and greeting of new prospects who themselves can become part of your network. The recognized need to establish contacts at the show is one of the primary reasons people attend.

ECRM has a vastly different format. They provide a one on one opportunity with decision makers for a fixed time – usually 20 minutes – to make your pitch and, you guessed it, make a new contact. You get to pick and choose who you want to meet with and, because they have their expenses paid by ECRM (and indirectly by you for exhibiting) the one on ones are mandatory. So if you have had difficulty in getting appointments with certain accounts, you now have the audience you've been trying to get. ECRM runs the gamut from tech to pet supplies so if it has to do with retail, they have an event for you.

Business Insider magazine recently wrote of a brand new global initiative that appears to be bypassing inept, willfully unconcerned, or non-existent government response to major disasters by taking matters into their own hands. And a very large prize awaits the team that comes up with the best solution. The initiative is calling for help from the software development community.

"Developers have revolutionized the way people live and interact with virtually everyone and everything. Where most people see challenges, developers see possibilities. That's why David Clark Cause® is launching Call for Code® alongside Founding Partner IBM®. This multi-year global initiative is a rallying cry to developers to use their skills and mastery of the latest technologies, and to create new ones, to drive positive and long-lasting change across the world with their code. The inaugural Call for Code Challenge theme is *Natural Disaster Preparedness and Relief.* The initiative would use cloud, data, AI, and blockchain technologies to create systems that allow for better responses to natural disasters around the globe."

"The main component of the initiative is a contest, where the creators of a prototype — like an app that predicts when and where the disaster will be most severe — will win $200,000, support from IBM to make the prototype a reality, and introduction to venture capitalists. IBM, which is working with the United Nations Human Rights Office and the American Red Cross®, is pledging $30 million over five years to the program. The money will go toward developer tools, technologies, free code and training with experts."

"Thousands of developers from around the world have already answered the call. More than 30 organizations are now signed up as program partners or affiliates, and more than 20 IBM clients have engaged their in-house developer teams to build solutions designed to help improve the current state of disaster preparedness. Call for Code has benefited from the support of generous celebrity supporters and content partners, as well as a panel of eminent judges who have volunteered to help select the winning technologies."

"Call for Code teams are already exploring effective ways to alert populations on evacuation procedures; ideas for getting real-time weather data to firefighters tackling wildfires; hurricane prediction and storm modeling solutions to better understand when to ask populations to evacuate coastal areas; and ways to help equip populations to survive the critical 72 hours immediately following an earthquake. Additionally, at a hackathon in Puerto Rico, a compelling idea named DroneAid was proposed, using drone and visual recognition technologies to help first responders identify areas and families in greatest need."

For the software community, the Call for Code Challenge represents networking at its finest, as teams combine their talents and strive to win a contest by creating solutions for natural disaster relief designed to benefit the entire world.

Networking successfully requires more than simply passing out business cards. All that does is deplete your supply of cards. Be honest, how many cards have you collected from individuals who you actually remember?

If you're serious about networking, the very first thing you need to do is watch and listen instead of talking. You'll want to learn what that person is looking for and why. Then you can determine whether you have a solution that might work. If you don't, you might be able to point that individual in the right direction, and leave a very positive impression as an opening for a follow-up opportunity to do business together.

Speaking of impressions...projecting a positive attitude is extremely important. Nobody wants to do business with someone who complains all the time. You'll need to be real. Don't pretend to profess interest in someone's business needs if you're just faking it for a sale. You won't be fooling anybody, and you'll never get another chance to sell anything to that client.

Your potential client is looking for the same thing you would be looking for, were you in his place. The client wants a trustworthy, dependable, straight-shooter. One who reliably and continually has the client's best interest in mind, and doesn't try to blow smoke.

Find your networking niche, enjoy what you're doing, do it right, and you'll expand your client list with people who will stick with you for years.

Information Resources;

Shriners International, Lions Club International, Rotary Club International, National Exchange Club, Kiwanis Club International, Optimist International, Call for Code, and Business Insider®

Dress For Wait...*WHAT?*

Chapter 16

Clothing Not Optional

Chapter 16

Clothing Not Optional

Dress for success has been around for a long time. Back in the day, the acceptable uniform for conducting business was a suit, or jacket and tie for men, and either pantsuits, dresses, or skirts and blouses for women. Easy. But, today's business world has gotten significantly more casual and, depending upon the business and location sector, you'll see shorts, t-shirts and sneakers or flip-flops.

My thinking has always been to be just a notch above, or at least equal to your client. If you come in wearing jeans and a T-shirt and your client is wearing a suit, guess what? You're starting off the conversation with disrespect and what's worse, an "I don't give a damn attitude." Clearly, it's not the best way to get a positive result. I've always felt that you should try to mirror the environment you're heading into. If the culture calls for a jacket and tie, you wear a jacket and tie. If instead, its jeans and T's, perhaps go with khakis and a button down shirt.

The point of the exercise is that you won't insult anyone by dressing up, but you certainly might, if you dress down.

Some thoughts on the way people dress came from a 2012 study published in the Journal of

Experimental Social Psychology. Maybe you'll agree, maybe you won't. Time moves so quickly these days that 2012 almost feels like a prior century. Here's what that 2012 study came up with.

1) Subjects who donned white lab coats (doctor style) scored higher on attention related tasks.

2) Designer labels are connected to financial success. It shows discipline, hard work and intelligence. Per Jennifer Baumgartner author of *You Are What You Wear.*

3) Kat Griffin founder of **Corporette.com** and owner of **Inside,** a wardrobe business in Washington: Clothing shows a commitment to your job. For young women starting out, an Hermes bag signals that you don't need to work. These days, wearing a suit is pretty much just for lawyers and politicians.

4) Rashini Rajkumar, Minneapolis-based executive coach and author of *Communicate That! : Your Toolbox for Powerful Presentations*. She coached executives not to wear their Italian leather shoes when they visit their factories. It's important to be seen as a "regular guy," she suggested. She also notes that a cool necklace can be a conversation starter.

5) **Nancy Connery** founder of **Connery Consulting a San Francisco consulting firm for technology**

companies: If you wear a suit, she cautions, tech companies will wonder if you can relate to the casual cult. Programmers are a different breed of cat.

Now those are interesting caveats. They're not chiseled in stone of course, and if you actually interview regular people, you might get a slightly different take on those pronouncements. Things actually change from year to year as well. And they change fast. We'll start with programmers.

In 2007, for example, a random commenter bewailed "I really want to know what it is about *programming*, or computers in general, that makes people want to grow a beard, have long hair, and dress like a slob."

By 2014, a mere seven years later, Stephanie Chan of ReadWrite was expounding upon a "Tech Uniform," and referencing the "studiedly casual California look associated with startup culture" referencing HBO's series "Silicon Valley" and films like "Social Network" and wondering whether reality was mirroring the Hollywood stereotype. She seemed to think the choice of clothing was "code—an algorithm designed around efficiency."

For early programmers, dressing for work used to boil down to rummaging in the dresser and grabbing whatever happened to be clean. OK, this may still be the case, but a fresh crop of

191

programmers are coming out of college and the look is no longer grunge.

"Perhaps it's the trickle-up effect within the tech community," she suggested. "Young startup entrepreneurs straight out of university carry their casual academic dress into the workplace, from whiteboard sessions to board meetings."

The fraternity crowd is looking to the guy at the top of the food chain who is now older and more sophisticated, and they unconsciously attempt to dress accordingly. The goal for many is not to spend their lives in ripped jeans, flip-flops and a logo t-shirt or branded hoodie, and despite the comfort level and you can still do a lot with a t-shirt.

The thing is, there's big money to be made in I.T. and talented programmers would like very much to have a shot at the brass ring, an objective which still remains very achievable.

Most angel investors are not wearing flip-flops. They're wearing suits and wingtips. And although they know talent when they see it, they also appreciate someone with judgment. If you're planning on wearing jeans, a rumpled t-shirt, sandals, and a three-day beard to an interview with potential financial backers, it might help if you also had the talent, I.Q. and business savvy of Bill Gates.

Now let's look at what, on the surface anyway, seems perfectly logical, the caveat for senior executives "not to wear their Italian leather shoes when they visit their factories," because "it's important to be seen as a "regular guy". The advice is sound, but the executive coach's reasoning is ridiculous.

If you're a senior executive wearing a $5,000 suit to tour the factory you're not going to be viewed as a "regular guy" by anybody. Even if you're wearing a well tailored $500 suit, the employees are going to judge you by what comes out of your mouth, and whether or not you know what you're talking about. It has absolutely nothing to do with what kind of shoes you're wearing. (And that goes for men as well as women.)

The number one type shoe to wear on any kind of factory floor is one that's slip-resistant. Depending upon what type of manufacturing is taking place in that factory, a slip resistant shoe, which may or may not be further equipped with a composite or steel-toe, has the potential to prevent an injury.

Any exec, male or female, whose position entails occasional visits to factories, already has a good looking pair of non-slip Italian leather dress shoes, (with, or without reinforced toes) in his or her closet for just such an occasion.

Darlene Price, president of *Well Said, Inc.* recently shared the fact that during her twenty-plus years as an executive coach, one of the biggest roadblocks to career advancement that she has identified, is inappropriate dress in the workplace.

There are between three and four different levels of business dress, depending upon how anal-retentive your company is, and there are scores of books and websites which purport to specify exactly what each means. Unless you happen to work for a Swiss company which has a 44 page dress code for employees, some basic common sense goes a long way in most companies in America.

We'll do men first.

Depending upon the degree of formality in your office here's what you'll be looking at. Mostly boring. OK, I was overly honest. But there's an upside I'll tell you about in a moment.

<u>Extremely formal, stultifyingly conservative workplace:</u>
Navy Blue, Black or Charcoal color suits having two or three button jackets, worn with a white or light blue long sleeve shirt, accented by boring solid color very conservative color ties with no patterns or designs, with or without optional boring cufflinks and/or tie clips. Black socks, polished black lace up shoes. Three piece suits with matching vests are included in this category but must never be worn without a tie. Pocket watches

with gold chains are generally considered overly flashy.

Wildly reckless conservative workplace: Navy Blue, Black or Charcoal color suits having two or three button jackets, worn with a white or light blue long sleeve shirt, accented by boring solid color very conservative ties *with* boring patterns or designs, and with or without optional boring cufflinks and/or tie clips. Discretely patterned socks, and polished black shoes may be augmented with either traditional loafers or conservative Italian leather ankle boots.

OK, I was kidding on the second one. It's not wildly reckless. It's just a step down from a seriously conservative workplace. You can add wild colors to the suit collection, like light gray, tan, and brown. If you're wearing a tan or brown suit, naturally you must wear brown shoes instead of black.

If you want to get totally wild you can pair a pair of light gray pants with a navy blue blazer that has gold buttons, plus a white or blue shirt and attractively patterned or striped tie. Actually this is a very nice look.

Now I did tell you that there's an upside. For some utterly unknown reason, women REALLY like well-groomed men who wear suits. They're especially fond of men who wear three piece suits and ties.

And EVERY man looks good in a decent quality suit.

One of the most memorable quotations from women about three piece suits is this; "The only thing sexier than watching a good looking man wearing a three piece suit, is watching a good looking man get out of a three piece suit."

You should write that down and have it laminated for your wallet.

Now then, let's discuss grooming for a moment. It's actually part of the dress code. *5 o'clock shadow* was only attractive on one person in the entire world, and that was Don Johnson when he drove a Ferrari® and starred in *Miami Vice* starting back in 1984. Go ahead and count how many years ago that was. Also I have it on good authority that razor burn is not romantic. If you're trying to grow a beard, do it on vacation and make sure it's properly shaped and groomed by the time you return to work. Go easy on the after shave or cologne. Good personal hygiene is expected to be maintained.

Shaggy hair and long beards are best reserved for Santa Claus and Grizzly Adams. Pony-tails and man-buns are equally faddish and not particularly attractive to women or to your boss. Trust me on this. I took a poll.

Casual dress for men does not mean mesh t-shirts, gym shorts and flip-flops.

According to the University of California at Riverside, business casual for men generally means a button-down or polo shirt, and/or a pull-over cardigan. Khakis, Dockers®, or corduroy pants are also good. Sport coats are encouraged. Belts and shoes must match. Lace up leather shoes and loafers are fine. Belts, shoes and dark socks are expected to compliment the overall outfit.

You'll notice that tennis shoes, cowboy boots, flip-flops, and sandals were not included. Skip short sleeve shirts with a tie, and please, no pocket-protectors. As might be expected, no shirts with logos, wrinkled clothing, or denim jeans.

The Society for Human Resource Management reminds you that the list of inappropriate casual wear includes muscle shirts, along with camouflage and crop tops. If t-shirts are permitted to be worn on certain occasions, shirts emblazoned with inappropriate slogans are not.

Now then, we may as well tackle what we've seen in the way of corporate dress codes for women.

Once upon a time, an Hermes bag signaled that you didn't need to work. Today, however, there are an abundance of websites which rent designer clothing and accessories. Women are simply going to have to be judged by their brains instead of their perceived wealth vis-à-vis their clothing.

Now about those corporate dress codes: Jewelry – The general rule of thumb in the corporate world is to skip the dangly earrings and keep remaining jewelry at a minimum. Engagement and wedding rings, right hand ring, watch, and simple necklaces are fine. Statement necklaces in good taste which compliment the outfit are acceptable. Visible tattoos are prohibited, as are visible piercings, beyond two per ear. Underwear is required to be worn. No kidding, that actually had to be said.

Grooming:

Employees are expected to have clean, neatly trimmed and well manicured nails with or without clear or traditional solid color nail polish and without further design embellishment. (i.e.- No two inch long multi-color nails covered with sequins.) Good hygiene is expected to be maintained.

Neatly groomed hair without statement dye colors. Discretely applied daytime cosmetics. A bare minimum of perfume or cologne.

Clothing guidelines for women are not that different than professional clothing requirements for men.

Skirts should be no shorter than slightly above the knee. No sleeveless dresses or blouses unless worn under a blazer. Conservative scarves are permitted. No bare midriffs, no jeans, no open-toed shoes.   O.K. that last one is just plain weird. Women have worn conservatively-styled peep-toe and/or sling-back shoes with business suits since the 1940's.   But corporate H.R. seems to have ruled them out in the 21'st century.

Appropriately tailored dresses or pantsuits in solid conservative colors are on the approved list. Solid color blouses and skirts, nothing ostentatious, nothing tight, or low cut, or off shoulder. No excessively high heels. Dress for work, not for the theatre or a cocktail party. No sequins or rhinestones. Do we really have to say that? Apparently.

No bare legs with dresses or skirts. Got that?   No bare legs. Stockings/Pantyhose in nude or suntan shades are required. Or tights in winter.

Well there actually is a benefit to pantyhose, and they do make legs look better, especially during winter months when your summer tan is long gone. They also smooth out clothing lines, since they have built-in underwear. There's also a medical benefit, especially if you fly a lot. They help prevent deep vein thrombosis.

But a long-standing complaint women have always had about pantyhose is that they're expensive. And they always, *always* get runs in them. A run in one leg means you have to toss the whole thing out. Otherwise women actually like them.

And now they're back in vogue, thanks to Prince William, Duke of Cambridge's wife Kate Middleton (Catherine, Her Royal Highness the Duchess of Cambridge) and her sister-in-law, Prince Harry's wife, Meghan Markle, Duchess of Sussex. Both young women dress to the nines, and interestingly enough, both are *mandated* by England's Queen Elizabeth to wear pantyhose.

Seriously. Not kidding.

Enter a solution. A start-up with an absolutely brilliant solution exceeded their $25,000. Kickstarter® goal. By a LOT. As of September of 2018 the sum of $190,073. had been raised.

For what? "The world's first pair of indestructible sheer tights. Revolutionary patent-pending design, made from fibers used in bulletproof vests." Really!

The web page states;

"Disclaimer: While Sheerly Genius® has been developed using ballistic grade fibers, the end product is not in itself bulletproof. These are for the boardroom, not the battlefield!

Wearing sheers shouldn't mean walking around with extra pairs, or clear nail polish. No one has time for that! After over a year of R&D, Sheerly

Genius has created the strongest sheer tights in the world. Sheerly Genius tights are not only reusable - but tested up to 50 wears!

Our patent pending design combines ballistic grade fibers (up to 10 times stronger than steel), with a proprietary knit and manufacturing process. Our fibers are so strong they actually break traditional pantyhose machines so we've retrofit machines specifically to work for our product."

Now *that* makes sense.

The only thing I'll leave you with for this chapter is an important warning.

During the same general time frame that Don Johnson as James "Sonny" Crockett, and Philip Michael Thomas as Ricardo Tubbs were tooling around Miami in their seriously cool white Ferrari Testarossa for the filming of *Miami Vice*, sheer blouses were all the rage.

Women often paired sheer blouses with sheer lacy undergarments, which meant that the outfits left little to the imagination.

The productive work-load dropped off considerably whenever any woman in an office wore a sheer blouse. Executives were themselves badly distracted.

The head of one of Miami's most exclusive real estate agencies, a charming Italian man from Milan, with an office full of attractive women and thoroughly distracted salesmen, finally called a sales meeting, and to the great amusement of the entire office, shouted…

"NO BOOBIE-LOOKING BLOUSES!"

Consider yourself warned.

Boobie-looking blouses are back in style.

Shit happens.
Face it head on.

Chapter 17

Courage Means Don't Let Fear Stop You

Chapter 17

Courage Means Don't Let Fear Stop You

Fear is one of the stronger motivational factors that drive all of us. Fear of losing a job, fear of injuring another (including hurting our loved ones), fear of being attacked, and fear of being found out for the weaknesses that we all have.

Fear is at the same time the *most* controllable and the *least* controllable emotion. It affects our behavior and influences others. Case in point; we all watched the evening news and saw otherwise normal people allow fear to eradicate the better side of our national character. We saw the specter of fear justify locking innocent children in cages (nearly 13,000 children remained imprisoned as of the third quarter of 2018. The number included nursing infants ripped from their mother's arms.)

Fear makes us less able to function as workers and as citizens. Fear inhibits rational thought. Fear makes people afraid to examine solutions based on reality.

Fear provokes division instead of unity, and perpetuates the myth that we need to position the communal wagons in an ever-shrinking circle. As that circle of wagons grows smaller, it forces us to recognize the stark division between yielding to a climate of fear and a determination to insist upon honor, reality and truth, as humanity's better choice.

We are faced with so much fear.

Fear of screwing up a presentation. Fear of not making enough sales. Fear of losing our jobs, fear of not finding another job. Fear of not having enough money to pay our bills, or to feed our family. Fear of illness, fear of hospitalization. Fear of having no insurance. Fear of being unable to pay for needed medicine. Fear of losing our homes. Fear of letting down those who depend upon us. Fear of losing our self-respect, fear of losing our sense of self.

How do we look after the concerns of others, if we cannot look firmly at our own wants and needs? How do we proceed? Where in the world do we even start?

Fear and the accompanying stress have a significant effect, both on our lives and our health. When we're overwhelmed with fear, crippled by stress, we find it difficult to concentrate. A certain mental paralysis that sets in, and at the end of the day we ask ourselves what we've accomplished, and we come up empty. A "plan B" eludes us.

Oftentimes although we had a perfectly good "to-do" list for that particular day, we found ourselves doing something else entirely. And while what we *did* do might have *seemed* important at the time, and it actually may have *been* important, the problem is that it didn't address the immediate task. We unconsciously shot ourselves in the proverbial foot. We can't get those hours back.

What we chose to do may have helped someone else, and that would have been a very good thing. But it wasn't what we needed to do *today*, and what we did do, albeit surely important to someone, somewhere, surely could have waited until next week.

In short, we have spent our entire suicidal day deliberately allowing ourselves to be nibbled to death by ducks.

The question is, why did we allow that to happen? Is there something we were afraid of? Were we seeking a brief respite from that underlying fear of failure by doing something that momentarily gave us pleasure, instead of engaging in a task we subconsciously associated with the necessity to address the problem at hand? Why would we do that?   Is it because we felt as if regardless of whether we did what was necessary or not, it would probably never be enough?

Are we actually pessimists, merely deluding ourselves into thinking we are optimists?

Or do we simply just hate what we're doing, and without realizing it, find that we're deliberately sabotaging ourselves? Are we generating our own fear?

Do we dream of ascending to a C-level position within the company we work for so we can turn that business around and make it really grow? Do we want to switch companies? Do we yearn to start our own business? Are we afraid to make our desires known for fear we'll lose what we already have? Are we constrained by fear of risking our family's financial security?

Perhaps it's time for us to lean back and allow ourselves to become introspective. To really sort through those fears and determine which ones have validity, which can be immediately overcome, and which fears simply need to be consigned to the dustbin.

Humans often tend to define themselves by their professions. Doing so occasionally allows us to use a minimum of words to sum up years of higher education and/or expert level, hands-on experience in the field of our choice.

When someone says "surgeon" or "veterinarian" or "lawyer" or "professor" or "nurse" or "architect" or "engineer" our minds generate a mental image. If we say "football player" or "basketball coach" or "kindergarten teacher" or "plumber" our minds do the same thing. When we say something like, "I'm in construction" or "I'm in marketing" or "I'm in real estate" or "I'm in electronics" or "I'm in I.T." or "I'm in hardware" we've used a nicely broad generality which encourages someone to inquire further and frequently makes a good conversation starter.

When you're introduced to someone and they ask "What kind of work do you do?" how do you reply? Is that an answer which pleases you? If not, what is it that you'd like to be able to say? Is fear holding you back from following a dream?

Thousands of self-help experts insist that there is power in positive thinking.

A significantly less number of experts suggest that positive thinking can actually produce negative results, but that seems to be limited to those individuals with negative, pessimistic personalities.

You already know how to recognize a negative, pessimistic personality. The Disney® character Eeyore is the perfect example.

"Good morning, Eeyore! It's a beautiful day for our picnic, isn't it?"

Eeyore would look around at the sunny day with bright blue skies and fluffy white clouds and reply morosely, "Yes, but it will probably rain and spoil everything."

Fortunately, positive thinking seems to be extremely beneficial to people with a positive outlook on life, and happily, there are an abundance of optimists.

Attitude is everything. "I have a pretty good head on my shoulders, and I know how to do this. People seem to like me, and I enjoy what I do. I will put my mind to doing this thing and I absolutely *will* get it done. I can *do* this." Self-reinforcement really *does* work.

There is no "fate dealt me a lousy hand" excuse involved here. There is no fear. This is a matter of self-determination. You really CAN do this. You really CAN overcome fear. You absolutely CAN eliminate fear and move forward with your objective.

One way to overcome fear is to put it into perspective. Understand that unpleasant things can indeed happen, scary things can happen, but we don't have to wallow in fear. We can be aware of it, set it off to one side and continue working toward our objective, keep driving toward our ultimate goal. Working toward what needs to be done, working towards what we want to get done, working toward accomplishing our hopes and our dreams, is what we *need* to do. We can get past whatever the current problems are. We can _DO_ this.

A true story: A few years back, when a new man had just been appointed to the Deanship of the prestigious University of Pennsylvania Medical School, the incoming Dean decided to modify a couple of features in his office. Chief among them, the most important element he wanted to see remodeled in his office sounded fairly mundane, albeit admittedly quite unusual.

The Dean sketched out what he wanted done, then authorized the replacement of the large section of the painted metal pipe which was situated along one wall of his office. Up until that point, the painted pipe had been all but invisible in his office. It had simply blended into the background. Handsome bookcases and framed photographs, diplomas and various awards drew a visitor's eye away from the pipe which had been painted the same color as the wall.

The workmen who arrived in his office to receive the Dean's instructions remained utterly baffled by his request. There was certainly nothing wrong with the existing pipe. Privately they inquired of each other if they thought the Dean knew what he was doing. Nobody had a clue, and naturally they were a bit hesitant to question their new boss, who happened to be incredibly bright, so... figuring there must be a perfectly good reason for his decision to do this, they simply shrugged their shoulders, followed his instructions and got to work.

Truth be known, the instructions he gave them really were quite strange.

The Dean had instructed the workmen to replace the existing large painted metal pipe with an equally large transparent Plexiglas® pipe instead.

The previously unobtrusive length of painted pipe was gone, replaced with what was now enormously noticeable, because the new pipe, as clear as the walls of an aquarium, ran all the way from the ceiling, on down the wall directly behind his desk, and then through the floor.

Fortunately, the workmen were able to seamlessly and successfully connect the clear pipe with the traditional painted metal pipes located on the floors both above and beneath his office.

What was downstairs? Just offices, which still retained their painted metal pipes. What was upstairs? Directly above the Dean's office was a very large laboratory.

The new Plexiglas® pipe was now connected to the cleanout drain for the animals quartered on the floor above, and when cages were cleaned, the detritus was washed down the drain. The flushed water descended through clear pipes in the Dean's office then continued all the way down through painted metal pipes on the floors below. The newly installed clear pipe now offered an up-close, personal, and very obvious view of the animal waste that was being propelled in very large and decidedly off-putting quantities past the Dean's office and on down to the drain field.

The Dean wanted to constantly, albeit humorously, continue to remind students, faculty, cohorts, and visitors alike, of what always flowed downhill, what had to be cleaned with regularity and, he wanted to graphically demonstrate the intrinsically humble nature of the most functional of tasks.

Without resorting to the installation of transparent pipe, we too can profit from the example set in place. Our ability to put things into perspective will keep us from being overwhelmed by fear. Humans are inherently courageous. We're hard-wired for courage. Courage allows us to replace fear of the unknown, replace fear of retribution, and overcome fear of failure.

Shit happens. Often a whole heck of a lot of it comes down the pipe at once. But we don't have to let it overwhelm us. We can see it coming, we can watch it enter our lives. And we can watch it fade away. In the interim, we have the ability to put that deluge into perspective.

Take a step back and look at the big picture. We know how this is going to turn out. We've seen this movie before. That stuff is going to make terrific fertilizer, and it will end up growing some fantastically beautiful flowers.

Don't be Eeyore

Chapter 18

B+

Chapter 18

B+

No it's not a grade from school, but rather it means Be Positive. *The Power of Positive Thinking* that Dr Norman Vincent Peale wrote about back in 1952 still rings true today. Even the Mayo Clinic recognizes just how important positive thinking is to one's quality of life.

"Health benefits that positive thinking may provide include:

- Increased life span
- Lower rates of depression
- Lower levels of distress
- Greater resistance to the common cold
- Better psychological and physical well-being
- Better cardiovascular health and reduced risk of death from cardiovascular disease
- Better coping skills during hardships and times of stress

It's unclear why people who engage in positive thinking experience these health benefits. One theory is that having a positive outlook enables you to cope better with stressful situations, which reduces the harmful health effects of stress on your body.

It's also thought that positive and optimistic people tend to live healthier lifestyles — they get more physical activity, follow a healthier diet, and don't smoke or drink alcohol in excess."

I had a buddy who felt so strongly about positive thinking that he made up buttons with B+ on them. He was running for local office in the city I was living in and it became his rally point when he spoke to constituents. He won.

My buddy was absolutely correct, and some scientific studies appear to bear out his opinion.

The body replaces roughly one percent of its cells each day. That equates to roughly 30% of our cells being replaced by a month from now. So by a mere three months from now, we'll have already replaced all of the cells which are in our body today.

This time frame is particularly interesting, because it takes, on average, approximately three months for humans to make a change in their life, regardless of whether it's a lifestyle or habit. What's even more intriguing, is the fact that the cell's pace and form of renewal are not pre-determined. Instead, it appears that the level of cellular change can actually be influenced by our emotions.

What this research appears to suggest is that how we choose to live our lives actually has the ability to determine our futures.

As noted, this is not a new theory. Dr. Norman Vincent Peale wrote "The Power Of Positive Thinking" back in 1952. His book spent a whopping 186 weeks on the New York Times Best Sellers List, and was eventually translated into more than 40 languages. That theory certainly worked out well for Dr. Peale, didn't it?

Peale wrote that "The mind controls how the body feels; thus, letting go of negative energy and emotions will give infinite energy..." and "Happiness is created by choice, worrying only inhibits it and should be stopped. The next step in thinking positively is to always believe in success and not to believe in defeat because most obstacles are *mental in character*"

Like anything else of course, the mere idea that positive thinking can influence the directions one's life can take, is often angrily discounted.

(Mostly by people with lousy dispositions.)

Here's an interesting anecdote about positive thinking:

In the mid-1980's MetLife (Metropolitan Life Insurance) took stock of their hiring, sales, and employee retention figures. They weren't wild about what they saw. The cost of training a new employee was running $30,000. The company was hiring 5000 people a year. Half of the company's new hires quit within the first year, and four out of five were gone after the first four years. These were not happy numbers for the company's bottom line.

MetLife's CEO contacted psychologist Dr. Martin Seligman at the University of Pennsylvania and invited him to study the impact of optimism in people's success on MetLife's new hires. It represented a terrific opportunity for a large scale study. Seligman accepted the assignment and tracked 15,000 of MetLife's new hires, each of whom had been asked to take two tests, the company's regular screening exam, and Dr. Seligman's profile, the latter of which measured the employee's level of optimism.

Among those who were hired were some individuals who would not ordinarily have been hired, since they had flunked the company's regular screening exam. However they had scored quite high on Dr. Seligman's optimism test. For tracking purposes the individuals in that group were classified as "super-optimists."

Interestingly, those "super-optimists" did the best of all, outselling the pessimists in the first year by 21% and by 57% in the second year.

Seligman then suggested that MetLife hire only those individuals who had high levels of optimism. It made sense. The hires that scored in the top 10% of optimism sold 88% more than those who ranked in the most pessimistic 10%.

Additionally, by dividing the group into two parts, half optimists and half pessimists, over a two year study, it was determined that the optimists sold 37% more than the pessimists.

In 1995 Dr. Seligman expanded his study across a variety of different sales fields, ranging from insurance, real estate, car sales, and office products, to the field of banking. The final results showed that optimists outsold pessimists by a range of 20% to 40%.

One particularly extreme result was in the real estate industry, in which it was found that the most optimistic of agents sold *three times more* than the pessimistic agents.

The good news is that while optimism is innate, it can also be learned, providing results which help an individual to be come more productive, more confident, and most important, happier.

In an article for Harvard Business School, Professor John A. Davis, who studies family businesses, is quick to point out that pessimists also hold a valued place in business. "Pessimists can make good operational leaders," he reminds us. "But pessimists in the corner office or leading the family (business) are less likely to foster a culture of growth, risk taking, and wealth creation."

Insofar as the anticipated lifespan of optimists vs pessimists, the results are literally all over the map, with multiple studies targeting various gender and age groups.

For all intents and purposes, however, it all pretty much boils down to getting a decent night's sleep on a regular basis, taking care of yourself and gearing toward a generally healthy lifestyle, which means quit smoking, drink moderately, take it easy on the caffeine, get a reasonable amount of exercise, and try not to snarf down a half-gallon of ice cream every night. It looks like the Mayo Clinic was right.

In addition to optimism, the level of happiness in your life also enters into the equation, both for lifespan and for maintaining a positive attitude. But what is it that generates happiness?

Having enough money to pay the bills is pretty helpful, of course. Sometimes easier said than done, which might be a sign that a change of employment, or perhaps a change of career is something that might be lurking in the back of your mind. Perhaps it's time you asked yourself some questions. Are you happy in your current career? Do you look forward to going to work? Is it challenging? Is it intellectually satisfying? Do you enjoy camaraderie with those with whom you work? Do you have fun with what you do? Food for thought.

What's your relationship status? Not just a romantic relationship, but family and friends. Is there a social group composed of people whose company you enjoy? If you can't get out to physically socialize very often, is there an online group you enjoy conversing with? Perhaps there are people with similar likes or hobbies? That works too. Social interaction with friendly people can function as an emotional safety net, and in doing so, those relationships increase a positive attitude, which is good for you. Got a Facebook® page? Do you carefully research people before you automatically accept a friend request? Are you selective when it comes to accepting requests? Do you look at their page to see what it is that drew them to you in the first place before accepting that request? Do you recognize each of them when they post something? Do you find yourself caring and congratulating them when they post a small triumph? Do they care about your small triumphs? Social interaction is healthy. It's positive.

Little acts of kindness also generate a positive attitude. Holding a door open for someone is an act of kindness. If a child sitting in a grocery cart smiles and says "Hi!" the simple act of smiling back and saying "Hi!" in return makes you, the child, and the child's parent happy. It's a small kindness, but it leaves you with a positive feeling.

When was the last time you simply stopped to smell the roses? Do you go to work, come home, eat dinner, and turn on the TV? When was the last time you just walked around your own yard, stopped to admire the trees, or plant a flat of vegetables or flowers? When was the last time you sat outside looking at the moon while listening to the crickets? When did you stop at the mailbox to chat with a neighbor? Slowing down to enjoy the simple things that make you happy is another way to reinforce your positive attitude.

Exercise is something else that has a positive effect on your attitude. It's not only good for your body, it's also good for your head. Your body responds positively to increased blood circulation, and to using your muscles. Exercise also helps sharpen your mind.

Spending time with close or casual friends whose company you enjoy is a positive activity. Going out to dinner, catching a movie, going dancing, going for a sail, hitting the flea market, having a barbecue, all are good for a positive attitude.

Meditation? The act of meditating absolutely helps build a positive attitude.

Fun is also a terrific way to reinforce a positive attitude. Of course your idea of fun might not be the same as that of your friends or siblings. Everyone is different. Indulge your passion! Fishing, bird-watching, woodworking, sculpting, skiing, skating, surfing, kayaking, climbing, drawing, painting, writing, reading, racing, tennis, basketball, football, bowling, gardening, quilting, sewing, and lots more.

What's more, even the very act of buying things which are *related to* having those experiences also generates a positive attitude. So if you buy a fishing pole, or a book, or a tennis racquet, or a flat of flowers, or a frame to hang your painting, anything actually, just as long as it has to do with an experience you enjoy, even further enhances your happiness and in turn, your positive attitude.

Who knew?

Sources:
Mayo Clinic – Stress Management
Seligman Study Source: True Colors PEOPLE Solutions.
Source: NAV: Why Optimists Make More Money Than Pessimists
Independent.co.uk – Science: Happier People Have Things In Common

Reach Out And
Touch Somebody*

*Make sure you have permission

Chapter 19

Make It Personal

Chapter 19

Make It Personal

It's difficult to train employees. Teaching them to use the customer's name three times during any transaction, whether face-to-face or over the phone, that's certainly simple enough, but, it takes practice and persistence to be sure that the rule is consistently followed. And of course, follow-up is itself important.

Why does this rule get so much attention in business? That's simple. People want to be identifiable, and their name is the safest, simplest way to emotionally reach every individual person. That is to say, their name is the central part of not only who they are, but what they are in any particular circumstance.

From the time we were infants we learned to identify our parents using a very basic test. We relied upon smell, feel, and visual appearance. These were usually the first people we saw in the morning and the last people we saw at night before going to sleep. Their smell, feel and appearance were imprinted upon our infant brains. We learned where we belonged.

The next step for us was to be assigned a name; effectively a call-sign which separated us from a herd made up of others not all that different from ourselves. But it began to define who we were. Our name became special.

There are scientific studies performed during MRI tests, demonstrating brain activation when we hear our own name spoken. There is also evidence that children under sedation respond selectively to the sound of their own first name.*

Hearing our names spoken is important to our personal sense of worth. We appreciate that small courtesy from others. It makes us feel valued when someone has taken the time to remember us.

Likewise, one of the simplest ways for us to make a friend, acquaintance or client feel recognized, is for us to quickly recall and then speak their name aloud.

Remembering names, and especially linking names to faces can be a challenge for many people. Studies show that an amazing 85% of people 45 and older struggle to remember names and faces of not only clients and new acquaintances, but of people they've known for years, but may not have the opportunity to interact with on a regular basis. But it frequently happens to much younger people as well.

The inability to remember a name can be awkward, frustrating, and hugely embarrassing, and even worse, there's the very real potential for insulting the person whose name we have momentarily forgotten.

We can solve this. Our brains are learning machines, the more we use them, exercise them, the better they perform. Providing our brains with new challenges helps to build up our cognitive reserves. Social interaction and mental exercises tend to switch the brain into learning mode, thus both represent positive steps to help us keep our memories sharp.

One of the biggest problems with remembering names and faces is the fact that an introduction is often so brief and a follow-on conversation so distracting, that we inadvertently forego the opportunity to commit the name and other pertinent information to memory.

The **BBC** offers the following shortcut, which I have paraphrased below:

"The technique is designed to help you make a memorable connection between the face you're looking at and the name someone has just mentioned during an introduction. It may take a little effort at first, but once you've mastered it, you'll be able to respond faster and faster, and you'll soon find that it is almost as if people have their names tattooed on their foreheads. Here's how to go about it:

Step One
It might seem obvious but PAY ATTENTION when you're told the person's name.

Step Two
It's good to hear the name more than once. So you could get the person to repeat it – or you repeat it. Perhaps ask a question.

Step Three
Think: what does that name remind you of? The name 'Cathy' for example, might remind you of a cat.

Step Four
Now have a close (but subtle) look at the person's face and decide what appears to be their most noticeable bodily feature. It could be their smiling eyes or their nose, or freckles or a beauty spot.

Step Five
Now use your imagination to link the name with the person's most noticeable feature. If Cathy has a lot of little smile lines around her eyes for example, you could imagine cat whiskers. If possible, make the link memorable! Link the color of the cat in your mind to the color of Cathy's hair. Give the cat Cathy's hairdo. Picture a bewhiskered cat with Cathy's hair and smiling eyes. Make your visual links funny, bizarre, even weird – it doesn't matter, it's all good.

Step Six

Next time you see her, quickly scan her face, look at the color and style of her hair, see those little smile wrinkles around her eyes, and the image of whiskers will pop into your head. The image of a cat will flash through your mind and you'll remember the name prompt, cat...Cathy."

There's also a simple Brainsmart® game on the BBC website which allows visitors to test and build up their ability to connect names to faces. You have test choices that range from Easy to Medium to Hard. It's a very good place to start. http://www.bbc.co.uk/scotland/brainsmart/games/faces/

In the business world we often find ourselves confronted with clients experiencing a wide variety of moods during any given period of time. They might be happy, or sad, neutral, or even angry. Instinctively we wonder, and often react, as if their mood is somehow related to our company's products or our services. But it shouldn't really be that much of a surprise to learn that bottom line, although a client's comments might be peripherally related to our products or services or even the attitude of one of our employees, what's really important is not us, it's them.

What they really care about is themselves, their hopes, their dreams, their aspirations. In short, they want to feel as if, regardless of what they have to

233

say, they are not simply invisibly important to a company sensitive to client concerns, they are actually *individually* important and therefore recognizable to us. Whatever the situation, we need to remember to reinforce that fact that they are not just a number on an invoice, they're a real person to us. And to do so, it all begins with their name being spoken out loud (at least three times) but genuinely, actually caring, and as part of the conversation, not as if one were following a script.

Starting with this simple and basic starting point, we can begin to understand each client as being nominally alike while at the same time, recognizing that they are all different from one another. They all have the same expectation of their future transactions with us working just as they should, because we do care about client satisfaction, and we make a point of proving it by recognizing them personally. We use their name. Then we do it again. And again. We help them learn to trust us, and we make it a point of honor never to let them down.

Does it help? Of course it does. Think about being one of a nameless, faceless crowd, a soul trying to cope with a desire, or with a mundane chore that is considered important, either to them or to someone else that they care about.

You are the one who can make a difference in their life when they need a helping hand. You not only identify who they are, you use their name over and over again. It's your job to make them like, and appreciate your sincerity. We're basically tasked with freeing their spirit, inspiring their genius for living, simply by solving a problem that's preventing them from going on with their busy lives and addressing other, more pressing concerns. We do this by actually caring about solving their problem, or answering their questions, maybe briefly commiserating with them, or simply making them smile.

Sometimes that's not easy, and even congenial name repetition can't break through that short-tempered, annoyed, or angry client's barrier. You may have a terrible memory for names, it does happen. Some of us do have that as a drawback. If we're faced with an annoyed client it can become an even greater challenge just trying to commit their name to memory, much less deal with the task of getting them to settle down long enough to determine what's needed from you, in order to begin to address their problems.

It's of paramount importance not to respond to an angry insult with anything but understanding and patience, even if a client's anger seems to have suddenly been transferred to you personally. The instinctive urge to snap back with a short-tempered reply solves nothing, it only makes matters worse. We need to make it a point to take the high road while committing the client's name and face to memory and remembering to continue to use their name.

When this chapter opened, I said that making it personal was simple, and at the same time important. And so it is. There is a simple test that can be used to evaluate your judgment as it relates to this area. It is to determine in what specific situations would the way you personally feel, work *for* you, or *against* you.

Sometimes we can be our own worst enemy.

Think back. Have you ever been so uncomfortable with the idea of having to confess to a client that you literally forgot something you absolutely knew was critically important to them, and as a result you procrastinated facing them, which only made matters worse? Ouch.

Perhaps you failed to provide that timely solution the client needed to resolve a problem he or she desperately cared about. Maybe that was because either you didn't know what was needed, or you just hated the idea of having to ask for help from an unpleasant co-worker.

Perhaps your component supplier is going to be late with a delivery. You missed a great chance to resolve a problem earlier, maybe to request a delivery extension for your own product, because you were so afraid the client's response when you asked if that might still work for them, would be so volatile, that you put off dealing with the situation entirely, hoping somehow it would all go away.

Possibly you ignored the way a client or colleague felt about what you considered to be a minor issue. You avoided confronting the matter because it just wasn't that important to you. But one day the client or colleague's frustration surfaced, in an unpleasant manner. That meant that you were now faced with a much bigger problem, one which required especially delicate diplomacy, along with a healthy serving of mea culpa.

Taken together, (or separately) it all means you need to try very hard to understand exactly how the person you're about to deal with feels about a specific matter. It was important to them then, it's even more important to them now. That means it must also become important to you. This isn't something new. Look at it as an opportunity to learn from an unpleasant experience. Come away from it smarter and better equipped to handle problems in the future. Facing a problem now is always better than trying to face it later. It really is an old problem. It's also an old solution. It requires learning to treat people the same way you would appreciate being treated yourself.

Listening carefully is possibly the most desirable trait one can develop. Do you give someone the chance to vent, or to define their view of a specific problem?

Do you know how to put yourself in another's shoes? It's a gift, but it can also be taught. It allows you to feel the client or co-worker's satisfaction, confusion, or discontent. Quite often, the very best alternative is to listen very carefully so that you fully understand the situation and to say nothing at all. Merely nodding and agreeing nonverbally while making eye contact, can often be the most soothing alternative.

It's true that sometimes you just cannot satisfy the demands you're faced with. In that instance the very best answer is simply to be honest. Perhaps their request requires assistance that cannot be given without additional guidance from senior management. Perhaps the suggestions that have been offered to you by a co-worker or supervisor are things that you have already tried, and they just didn't work. Those attempted solutions failed to meet either the needs of the client or the traditional problem-solving resources currently at your disposal. The truth is still the best answer with which to provide them.

Tell them the situation as you know it to be, tell them you'll take it all the way to the top if need be in an attempt to get the proper answer for them. Let them know you really do care enough to go above and beyond. And then follow through with your promises and keep them in the loop with frequent status reports while that's happening.

Over your career you may have run into hundreds of client resistances to your attempts to help. There are also comments which you may find offensive, born out of client frustration or personal problems which may have absolutely nothing to do with the matter at hand, they've simply exacerbated the client's foul mood.

All of these situations fall into an entirely separate category, but that doesn't lessen their importance. Learn to treat them with great care. They are the issues which will reflect upon your current position in your company. Your decision to respond with a diplomatic or abrupt handling of that client will go a long way in determining whether you can look forward to a bright future with that firm, or if you should perhaps anticipate a change of employment, a little sooner than you had originally planned.

All matters having to do with customer relations, and with corporate relations will fall into the category of making it personal. You *are* the face of your company. You *are* the one who can make it personal for the client, personal for the situation, and most importantly, personal for you.

The way you treat others leaves an indelible mark upon your reputation. It is something that is taken into consideration when you are evaluated for promotions and raises. Your ability to make it personal, to really care about other people is as valuable to you as gold.

Your reputation will follow you throughout your entire professional career. You have in your hands the ability to increase your own value on a daily basis. If you seek a promotion, your track record precedes you. If you eventually decide to go out on your own, you'll have already established your positive reputation.

You are, to yourself, like money in the bank.

*https://www.ncbi.nlm.nih.gov/pmc/articles/PMC1647299/

Buckle up Sunshine,
We can do this.

Chapter 20

Get Smart

Chapter 20

Get Smart

One of the most difficult intangibles we often face is that of excellence, and our perception of it. We're in the trenches every day. We see what's needed. Yet for some reason, often what we suggest would be necessary to accomplish our goals falls upon deaf-ears. We try reframing our suggestion and yet, often our idea is allowed to fall by the wayside, or it is deliberately kicked aside.

We evaluate what can be done, and feel frustrated that it's not already being acted upon. Our idea seems to offer such a simple fix.

It's not an unusual problem.

The fully trained former student who excels in his field cannot find work, and as a result, he or she is confronted with a future which appears to be particularly bleak.

Every one of us, at one time or another, has witnessed a store clerk who cannot seem to add or subtract in order to simply make change. This is first grade arithmetic yet the clerk seems completely out of his or her element. Amazingly, today it takes a calculator to do what was historically not even considered to be a problem.

A trip to the bank to pick up a cashiers check can today be equally befuddling. One normally pulls out a checkbook, writes a check for the amount needed plus the bank charge, and passes it to the teller... who more often than not in today's environment picks it up, and looks at it blankly, literally unable to read it. "I'm sorry," the teller apologizes, "I don't know what this says. I can't read cursive." The bank customer looks up at the teller and blinks, totally aghast at what they've just heard.

How is this even possible? More pointedly, how could a bank teller possibly even have been hired with such a basic educational deficiency. What are the employment requirements at a financial institution for an employee who daily represents the face of a neighborhood bank and is called upon to cash checks or deposit funds? It boggles the mind.

Let's take one step further back and ask by what possible lapse in common sense would the ability to read and write in cursive, the very form in which the Constitution of the United States and the Bill of Rights are written, have been deliberately deleted from the curriculum of our elementary schools? By what logic would we no longer teach basic arithmetic? Whose idea was it to aggressively promote the dumbing-down of America? Did no one bother to think ahead?

Common core standards included a requirement for instruction in keyboarding, but did not mandate the teaching of cursive handwriting. As of 2013, California, Idaho, Indiana, Kansas Massachusetts, North Carolina and Utah, only seven states out of 50, had recognized the importance of cursive handwriting and elected to maintain its teaching.

"The original (Common Core curriculum) objective of bringing substandard schooling up to that of wealthier school districts seems to have been completely abandoned, and the budget for education has been repeatedly slashed." -*Source: Quora – Rosemary E. Williams*

We see workers who are staggeringly under-trained, or embarrassingly over-qualified for positions they currently hold, the latter forced to accept whatever was available simply to keep the lights on and pay the mortgage. This strikes all of us as absurd.

We live in a very strange world today, and we are in an equally strange position.

We expect everything we buy to function just as described, all the while facing the reality that the widget we acquire quite often falls well short of perfection – the result of misleading ads coupled with inferior materials and sub-standard workmanship.

We demand excellence, yet even our automobiles arrive with what we perceive to be absurd functional imperfections. Curiously, manufacturers continue to add ever more complex bells and whistles, many of which are doomed to eventual failure, saddling unhappy consumers with very high price tags for their repair.

It has become normal to disparage *Made in China* as a symbol of poor quality and short term product life. Yet, the number and complexity of manufactured goods from China continually increases without any of the time and testing needed to ensure that fine quality and well trained workmanship are present. Naturally, items that are made in the U.S. are far more expensive than those produced in off-shore, low labor cost countries, but quality is similarly lacking.

We are continually deluged with poll numbers demonstrating that the U.S. education system has taken a nose-dive. It has standards which lag far behind the rest of the world in the fields of math and science. It is especially painful to witness when we realize that the United States formerly led the world in those fields.

"As recently as 1992 the United States was ranked No.1 in high school and college education. In 2009, the United States was ranked 18th out of 36 industrialized nations. Over that time, complacency and inefficiency, reflective of lower priorities in education, and inconsistencies among the various school systems contributed to a decline." *(Source – HistoryNet)*

We no longer adequately support our early education public schools, while at the same time we expend new levels of funding for the military-industrial complex and grant absurdly lavish tax cuts to those who truly don't need them.

Every year the World Economic Forum releases a report which contains the state of the world's educational systems. The ones who made it into the top three in 2016 were; (1) Finland (2) Switzerland, and (3) Belgium *(Source – Independent.co.uk – 2016)*

In 2017 the top three were (1) Norway, (2) Finland, and (3) Switzerland *(Source: https://www.weforum.org/agenda/2017)*

In the meantime, many regular middle-class American husbands and wives are forced to have second and even third jobs just to pay for ever increasing costs of food, clothing, and vehicles. Home acquisition has become a goal for the wealthy only, and a higher education has become nearly unobtainable for children of the average American family.

Everything costs more and more, and while employment reports show drops in percentages to all time unemployment lows, wages earned by American workers do not increase. The workers who are now shut out, were skilled at the levels of World War II but fall short when considering changes which have become today's norms.

Graduates are confronted with enormous debt due to a student loan program seemingly designed to disgorge large numbers of under-trained and over-trained students.

All are saddled with high levels of debt, and today's graduates find no work opportunities in the very fields they have studied and learned, nor can they find suitable employment that pays adequately so they can reduce their student loan debt. These now educated young people are ready to leave home. But instead, the current system forces them to continue to live under their parent's roof until many years have passed. They live with their parents because they cannot afford to be self-supporting.

The Atlantic magazine recently ran an article which stated that "Since 2013, the Federal Reserve Board has conducted a survey to 'monitor the financial and economic status of American consumers.'" What it found was appalling. "The Fed asked respondents how they would pay for a $400 emergency. The answer: *47 percent* of respondents said that either they would cover the expense by borrowing or selling something, or they would not be able to come up with the $400 at all."

What can be the next step(s)? It starts with raising the educational bar for the intellectually inclined students and creating employment opportunities for the others. There is no "time-out" for getting the orders necessary from Washington. There is the hope that the work-denied students of today will be able to find a future.

What does this mean? It is a difficult task for the student soon to graduate from college. He or she has skills for which there are few jobs available. Alternatives are limited for those that want to be in other than a health-related or hotel-oriented marketplace.

We already have more lawyers in this country than are necessary, an abundance of them are on cable television or in politically elected and support offices.

Physicians are specializing in arcane fields while the number of generalists shrink at the time when only complex diseases are driving customers to seek help. And for the medical practitioner, the governmental paperwork requirement is nearly as daunting as are the student loans for the few current arenas for jobs.

The future is both dim and bright. Some areas will succeed, grow, and develop. Many will languish and then disappear as the technology they are based upon proves to be incapable of supporting growth.

What were once traditional, readily available factory jobs are now no longer available. Vehicle manufacturing companies, and nearly all manufacture of broadly accepted widgets will soon be the purview of robotics and artificial intelligence fabrication.

Materials used will of necessity be those which are recycled and not damaging to the environment. Science will become more and more popular with substantial gains emerging in every field touched by expansion. There is likely to be growth and development in industries which will create the need for well trained technocrats, those who are able to remain current in a rapidly developing field.

One hopes that Government will become the purview of the informed and well-educated, instead of the greed infested playground of those who have entered the field of politics for personal profit and lobbyist payoffs. Similarly, we trust that real diplomats, those with intellectual gravitas, will once again appear, able to guide, adopt and adapt to the changing needs of not only our own nation, but developing nations, for the benefit of the entire planet.

There will be a rebirth in the face of our nation and of the world. That's the only way we can survive as species. We must help remake both our physical and intellectual environment so that Honesty, and with it Trust, will become the norm.

Today, we are also mired in the transition from a disposable society, in what we purchase, to the projected choices of tomorrow's enlightened society. The future mandates that this transition must not be driven by the greed and lack of concern prevalent today, but rather by the needs of the people of the entire globe. Society will grow and prosper. The transition is unlikely to be easy, but we must all work together to see to it that this *IS* what happens.

Our country gets an anticipated, nay, a hopeful grade of at least a B+ for the eventual outcome of what we will all inevitably encounter, suffer through, and through sheer determination, survive, during that momentous transition.

"We are committing ourselves to tasks of statecraft no less awesome than that of governing the Massachusetts Bay Colony, beset as it was then by terror without and disorder within. History will not judge our endeavors—and a government cannot be selected—merely on the basis of color or creed or even party affiliation. Neither will competence and loyalty and stature, while essential to the utmost, suffice in times such as these. For of those to whom much is given, much is required" – John F. Kennedy

"It was right here, in the waters around us, where the American experiment began. As the earliest settlers arrived on the shores of Boston and Salem and Plymouth, they dreamed of building a City upon a Hill. And the world watched, waiting to see if this improbable idea called America would succeed." Barack Obama

"These visitors to that city on the Potomac do not come as white or black, red or yellow; they are not Jews or Christians; conservatives or liberals; or Democrats or Republicans. They are Americans awed by what has gone before, proud of what for them is still… a shining city on a hill." – Ronald Reagan

Our goal is to come through all of this intact, as the shining COUNTRY on what must become a united planet.

ABOUT THE AUTHOR
Bruce Borenstein
Small Business Executive of the Year
Award Winner

Principal at <u>PH Advisors</u>

PH Advisors is a business accelerator which specializes in helping start-up companies to reach their milestones sooner.

Most recently, I was VP of Global Sales for **Nuheara** - a leader in the hearing health industry with their award winning *IQbuds*. I also served as a member of their Advisory Board. In my first year I directed sales upward of $5 million. Since then company has built upon the *IQBuds* foundation introducing new products into the market.

Previously, I held the position of President and CEO at **AfterShokz**. AfterShokz reinvented headphones with their bone conduction technology. I was responsible for all facets of their business including sales, marketing, operations, and finance. In their first five years I took the business from $0 to over $20 million. Some successful campaign that I directed included: an *IndieGoGo* campaign, a nationwide charity run partnered with the *United Relay of America*, and successful placement of product in over 400 retailers world-wide. I am pleased to say that AfterShokz has continued to grow and develop to this day.

Prior to AfterShokz, I was Executive Vice President of **The Neat Company**. Neat created proprietary software which integrated with scanners to digitize information on paper. This ground-breaking technology created an easier and more-efficient way for businesses and individuals alike to digitize financial documents. I was responsible for all sales - Domestic and International. I sat on the company's Operating Committee that set company strategy and direction.

Before joining Neat I was Principal and Sales Practice leader at *North Riverside Partners* a consulting firm specializing in assisting companies to gain market entry into the CE and Technology channel. Some clients included: **Shure Electronics, Richardson Electronics**, and **Time Pilot**.

DON'T BE A SCHMECKLE!

DON'T BE A SCHMECKLE!

www.ingramcontent.com/pod-product-compliance
Lightning Source LLC
Chambersburg PA
CBHW031532040426

42445CB00010B/495